Value Your Mate

Other books in the Strategic Christian Living series

Douglas McMurry and Everett L. Worthington, Jr., *Value Your Mate: How to Strengthen Your Marriage*

Daniel R. Green and Mel Lawrenz, *Why Do I Feel Like Hiding? How to Overcome Shame and Guilt*

James R. Beck and David T. Moore, *Why Worry? Conquering a Common Inclination*

Harold Wahking and Gene Zimmerman, *Fulfilled Sexuality: How to Find Help and Hope for Difficulties*

Siang-Yang Tan and John Ortberg, Jr., *Coping with Depression: The Common Cold of the Emotional Life*

Gary Steven Shogren and Edward T. Welch, *Running in Circles: How to Find Freedom from Addictive Behavior*

Mel Lawrenz and Daniel Green, *Life after Grief: How to Survive Loss and Trauma*

Everett L. Worthington, Jr., and Kirby Worthington, *Value Your Children: Becoming Better Parental Disciple-makers*

David Benner and Robert Harvey, *Choosing the Gift of Forgiveness: How to Overcome Hurts and Brokenness*

Rod Wilson and Glenn Taylor, *Exploring Your Anger: Friend or Foe?*

Value
Your Mate

How to Strengthen Your Marriage

Douglas McMurry
and
Everett L. Worthington, Jr.

 Baker Books

A Division of Baker Book House Co
Grand Rapids, Michigan 49516

Published by Baker Books
a division of Baker Book House Company
PO Box 6287, Grand Rapids, Michigan 49516-6287

Second printing, April 1997

Printed in the United States of America

Library of Congress Cataloging-in-Publication Data

McMurry, Douglas.
    Value your mate: how to strengthen your marriage / Douglas McMurry and Everett L. Worthington, Jr.
       p.   cm. (Strategic Christian living)
    Includes bibliographical references.
    ISBN 0-8010-9727-4
    1. Marriage—Religious aspects—Christianity. I. Worthington, Everett L., 1946– II. Title. III. Series.
BV835.M35   1994
248.8'44 dc20   93-36060

For current information about all releases from Baker Book House, visit our web site:
        http://www.bakerbooks.com

To my wife, Carla, who taught me much about relationships
—D. M.

For Mike and Kathy
—E. W.

Contents

How to Use This Book   9

1. The Valley of Trouble   11
2. The Pattern   21
3. Value   29
4. Faith in Jesus   37
5. Christianity   47
6. Core Vision of Marriage   55
7. Confession and Forgiveness   63
8. Closeness   71
9. Communication   81
10. Conflict Management   93
11. Cognition   103
12. Covenant and Commitment   115

Notes   125

How to Use This Book

We have designed this book as a help to couples who have entered into marriage counseling. However, it may also be used as a course of marriage renewal for couples who are not in counseling. It may enrich couples who would simply like to apply Christian teaching to their marriage.

Whatever your circumstances, we recommend that both partners purchase notebooks and use the questions scattered throughout the book to help you reflect on your marriage. We trust that, even if you are not going through marital difficulties, you may be enriched by the blueprint of Christ.

1

The Valley of Trouble

I (Doug) will never forget the evening when my wife Carla and I celebrated our twelfth wedding anniversary. We went to a local restaurant for dinner. A band was playing. Eventually word leaked out that Carla and I were celebrating a wedding anniversary. The lead singer embarrassed us by announcing our anniversary through the microphone, and he made us tell everyone which anniversary we were celebrating.

"Our twelfth," I said, half fearing that he was going to call us forward and exhibit us on stage like a rare archaeological specimen.

But he didn't call us forward. Neither did he treat our wedding anniversary like some quaint curiosity from the past. He acted as though a great miracle had just been performed between songs. He gasped: "Twelve years! How'd you do it? You don't hear about good marriages much anymore. You two deserve to be congratulated!" Everybody clapped. Enthusiastically, too.

A hodgepodge of emotions welled up in me, ranging from acute pride to devout humiliation. I wanted, all in a moment, to hide under the table and to stand on top of it. Then the lead musician told of how he had recently divorced his wife after only a few years of marriage. He was so candid and vulnerable as he described his disappointment and pain that, to this day thirteen years later, I have not forgotten it. It dawned on me that day that marriage—which I had always judged a rather ordinary, mundane matter—is in fact a heroic accomplishment. Yet the glory of our twelve-year accomplishment was marred by the pain we felt for countless couples whose marital hopes and dreams had disappeared, leaving a raw ache in their place.

That night, too, I saw so very clearly that most people—Christians and non-Christians alike—still hold to the marital dream, despite those among us who loudly and angrily belittle it. Most people want to " make it" with one faithful companion; want to raise a family in a secure home where they love and are loved; want this heroic accomplishment for themselves. They sense that marriage is preferable to a sequence of sexual encounters, the trauma of broken homes, or the sleaziness of phony intimacy peddled by jaded Hollywood film directors.

We firmly believe that most people want the secure intimacy of a stable marriage, and those who finally reject this hope do so because hurts and traumas have made it seem impossible. It is only after great struggle and much pain that we grudgingly settle for less.

The Breakdown of the Family

But many people *are* settling for less. The statistics on marital breakdown are no secret. Statistically, over half of all marriages will end in divorce.[1] Of second marriages, the probability of divorce is about two-thirds. The rate of failure for third marriages stands at about 70 percent. These figures show us that once the divorce ball gets rolling it is hard to stop. People who get divorced once are likely to get divorced again and again. Those who think that they "just picked a bad partner," and that the easy solution is to "pick a better one"—as though in a shopping mall—are undoubtedly deceiving themselves about why they are so unhappy in marriage. The problem is more likely to be traced to how they think about marriage and relate to their spouse. The effect of all these divorces on children has been catastrophic. After reviewing countless studies, Senator Dan Coates, a member of the Senate committee that deals with children and families, predicted that only 39 percent of children born in 1988 are likely to live with both parents until their eighteenth birthday. In three of five divorces, children are involved. Senator Coates says, " One study found that, 18 months after a divorce, children have a rate of sudden, serious psychological problems comparable to victims of natural disaster. Sixty-five percent of children—who had been functioning well before the divorce—couldn't concentrate in school, couldn't eat or sleep properly, couldn't make friends, were depressed, withdrawn or hostile. . . . The study's author concludes, 'Almost half of the children of divorce enter adulthood as worried, underachieving, and sometimes angry young men and women.'"[2]

Divorce, then, is not the answer it may seem to be— either for our own marital happiness or for our children. It is worthwhile to deal with difficulties in marriage, rather than to simply escape them through divorce and remarriage. "I'll try again with someone else" isn't the panacea that some people think it is.

Divorce may seem to be the easiest and least painful solution to a marriage problem. But it isn't even that, for in over half the divorces, it takes years to heal the scars of personal animosity, to deaden the pain of divorce settlements, and to get past the frustration of child custody disputes.

It isn't just for the kids' sake that we hope for an enduring marital love, but for ourselves, too. Marriage is a good plan, a rich possibility, if only we can make it work.

As I learned on my twelfth anniversary, God has placed in most of us a longing for a marriage where two people can energize each other with love. Here the stream of life constantly refreshes, no matter what happens in the world outside. In such a marriage, we hope to find a person who will stand by us, who will accept, forgive, respect, encourage, and cherish us totally—and vice versa. In the presence of this person we will be healed of life's earlier traumas. We will become strong and fruitful.

> **Question:** Do you share this hope of a love-sanctuary where two people can be secure in each other's presence? Why not take some time now to jot down (in a notebook, perhaps) the hopes and core vision that drove you to marry. What were you longing for? What were the ingredients of that vision? Get back in touch with your marital dream.

"I Want to Be Happy"

If, soon after marriage, I had put my marital vision into words, it would have focused almost entirely on my own sense of accomplishment in achieving marriage. At last I had found a woman who wanted to live with me. This seemed at the time like a great miracle too wonderful to believe. The acceptance of a living, breathing woman and the sense of achievement were what I was after. I thought little about the challenges this relationship would bring into my life or about the commitment I was making. I was incapable of discerning, even at age 25, what a challenge the marriage covenant is. I assumed that we would merely learn to be happy together, now that the hurdle of the wedding ceremony was successfully behind us.

Ah, but happiness was not so easily achieved. I remember back to the first years of my marriage—how Carla kept asking me "Do you love me?" several times a week. I reacted by telling her that I felt manipulated by her question. I didn't see how it could be very satisfying to her to have me answer "yes," since the "yes" was being wrenched out of me by force of her question.

A Cold Fish and a Bleeding Heart

What I couldn't see was that she needed me to communicate love to her more frequently than I was doing. To her my love was a food, not just optional vitamins. I was starving her. I was too absorbed in my own ambitions and experiences to pay attention to the underlying need that she was trying to show me.

Carla, in turn, began to reflect her unfilled hopes by criticizing me. One day, when I had just come home from the office, she lit in to me, with no apparent reason. She accused me of being a rotten father and husband. She said that she had been struggling with the needs of our two-year-old son, that she hated being trapped at home all day, and that I had been blind both to her and to Philip. Now, she said, when I came home, I always went down to my potter's wheel in the basement and completely ignored her. Didn't I realize that I had a family?

I didn't like her tone of voice, and I was hurt by her sarcasm. I had always taken pride in my abilities as a potter. Besides, pottery was relaxing after a stressful day at work. My natural response to conflict was to close people out of my life whenever they were unpleasant. I mumbled something and went up grudgingly to play with Phil while Carla put dinner on the table.

She didn't seem to appreciate me.

She didn't think that I appreciated her, either, but that was not what was foremost in my mind. What was foremost was that I didn't want her to lay into me like that again. She needed to be taught a lesson. She needed to know that she had made a mistake in condemning me for being a bad father and husband. I decided—almost without thinking about it—to give her the cold shoulder. My shoulders are skinny and bony and they turn cold fast and easy.

As I recall, that cold shoulder lasted several days. I did not reflect on whether this was the right response, whether it was how Jesus wanted me to behave toward my wife. The cold shoulder was what I had always served up on occasions of this sort—my natural way whenever I was faced with an unpleasant situation. I had been showing people cold shoulders for years. It didn't occur to me to ask whether I was right or wrong or what my options were. It was only later that it dawned on me that Jesus recommends a certain pattern of living, and that I needed to change my life to fit that pattern. Though I was a pastor, I did not yet realize that Jesus wanted me to apply his teaching to my personal life and to my marriage.

The Frivolous Day

There were two annual occasions that were important to my wife—more important even than her birthday. One was our anniversary, the other, Valentine's Day. I have never had any problem remembering and appreciating our anniversary. But Valentine's Day always seemed hopelessly frivolous to me.

Of course, by thinking of Valentine's Day in that way, I was missing the whole point of it. Valentine's Day was always important to Carla. On our first Valentine's Day she made me a heart-shaped jello. Unfortunately, she inadvertently bought sour cream *with chives* in it, which clashed with the cherry-flavored jello. We have joked about that first Valentine's Day fiasco ever since.

But she couldn't make a joke out of my persistent habit of doing nothing on Valentine's Day. Her attitude was, "Better to try and fail than not to try at all." It did not occur to me that she was once again asking me to communicate love. To her, Valentine's Day was a time-honored opportunity— a game in which the play is for real, not just for fun—to communicate love.

"Little Cupids shooting arrows through peoples' hearts have nothing to do with Christianity," I complained. "In fact, it's downright pagan." My protests kept me from seeing Christ's pattern, which could have been my salvation every Valentine's Day. This pattern could have kept my day from meltdown like soupy jello with chives in it, but I couldn't see it.

I resented Carla's unhappiness. It seemed to me unfair and unreasonable that she should be unhappy. She would look at me with her longest face, and I couldn't see why she had to make such a big deal out of trivial things like Valentine's Day. "She's just causing trouble," I mumbled to myself.

Bedtime Blues

Often she would bring up issues of conflict just after we had gone to bed. I had set the alarm, closed my eyes, and sighed a sigh of satisfaction, looking forward to the sweetness of dreamland. Then: "Doug, we need to talk." I couldn't believe it. How could she be so cruel, dragging me from my serenity into a heavy, stressful discussion of marital problems?

Yes, I knew the Apostle Paul had written, "Don't let the sun go down on your anger," and Carla was trying her best to follow this advice. But the sun had already been down many hours, and the last thing I wanted was a heavy, stressful discussion that would probably keep me tossing and turning past midnight.

Of course, it never occurred to me that, since my way of dealing with conflict was to escape to my soothing, hypnotic potter's wheel, Carla had no other convenient time to bring up issues that were troubling her. I merely reacted to her by complaining, "Carla, bedtime isn't the time to talk about it. If we do, I'll be upset and unable to get to sleep. And tomorrow I'll be cranky and won't be ready for ministry." Ha. I knew she wouldn't want to stand in the way of ministry.

I didn't know how to move through these issues by following the way of Jesus. Time and again I simply reacted to Carla in habitual, unreflective ways that could never resolve anything. In fact, my way of (not) dealing with Carla kept unresolved issues alive and seething just underneath the sheets more or less forever. My wife, whose heart was bleeding, was crying out for love from me, *The Number One Cold Fish of All Time.*

The Valley of Trouble

I wasn't enjoying these marital troubles. They were a far cry from the hopeful, peaceful vision that I had had in mind on my wedding day. Yet I could not ignore these troubles, because I was married to them. God had placed me in a situation where I had to face my inadequacy and stop running away to my potter's wheel and my office.

The very troubles I had to walk through became for me and for Carla a challenge to grow into a deeper kind of love and maturity in Christ. Without those troubles I would have missed a hundred mirrors to show me to myself, a hundred binding ropes to drag me to my need for God. I had to decide whether I wanted to learn how to love—and not just to preach about it on Sunday mornings. Trouble had become a teacher whose voice I could not ignore.

Through the prophet Hosea, God compared his relationship with Israel to a very unfulfilling marriage. But in the midst of the frustration of being married to Israel, he said, "I will allure her, and bring her into the wilderness, and speak tenderly to her . . . and make the Valley of Achor (Trouble) a door of hope" (Hos. 2:14, 15 RSV).

Trouble can be a door of hope, depending on how we respond to it. God leads us through the Valley of Trouble with hidden purposes in mind. Without the Valley of Trouble, most of us would learn nothing, would make no positive changes in character, would not become mature in Christ. God is eager to use our Valley of Trouble as a door of hope, as an opportunity for heroism.

Question: Insofar as you are reading this book, you are likely to be having struggles that hinder your marriage. But take stock: are there areas of hope, too? Are you willing to accept trouble as an invitation to learn some new patterns of relating to your spouse and vice versa?

Marriage Problems Are Everywhere

If you feel as though your marriage is not perfect, you are not alone. In preparation for this series of books, Baker Book House surveyed 405 pastors of every major denomination. In answer to the question, "What are the most common problems that you have had counselees bring to you," marriage problems took first place. Fully 84 percent of the pastors marked this box, with the next frequent problem being depression (64 percent), and the next, addictions (44 percent).[3]

Clearly, marriage is no easy challenge. Yet this challenge can be the stimulus to help us see areas of needed growth to which we have been blind. Nothing worth doing comes easy. But if we seek God's power and guidance to do a difficult thing—make marriage work—God can raise us up, revealing new vistas of what he promises to those who learn his ways more deeply.

2

The Pattern

To make a new suit, you not only need clear instructions, but you also need a pattern to sew by.

We believe that God has given a pattern by which we can build relationships, especially marriages. Following God's pattern can lead to the fulfillment of the marital vision.

In the sermon on the mount, Jesus said: "Everyone who hears these words of mine and puts them into practice is like a wise man who built his house on the rock. The rain came down, the streams rose, and the winds blew and beat against that house; yet it did not fall, because it had its foundation on the rock" (Matt. 7:24–25). Many people think Jesus was saying that we should go to church, hear his teachings, and try to understand them. We Westerners have built our culture on the assumption that if we comprehend a teaching with our minds, it will help us. But Jesus is telling us that perceiving his teaching with our rational minds will not necessarily do us any good at all. We must try his teaching out. To put down our Bibles and say, "Aha, that was an interesting word Jesus had there; it gave me a new idea to think about," is a very American thing to do. But it is also futile and unproductive.

Jesus has given us a pattern. If it is a pattern, then it has value only if we follow it in building our lives and marriages. It is an architectural plan. If we follow it in our building project, our marriages will survive the storms of life. If we want a marriage that does not fall apart at the first sign of serious storm, then we must be willing to take a close look to see if we are using the pattern of Christ.

The pattern of Christ is described frequently in the New Testament, and it is always the same wherever we look. It always includes the same two ingredients:

> For in Christ Jesus neither circumcision nor uncircumcision is of any avail, but faith working through love (Gal. 5:6 RSV).

> What you heard from me, keep as the pattern of sound teaching, with faith and love in Christ Jesus (2 Tim. 1:13).

Faith working through love. That is the pattern. The trick, of course, is to apply this pattern to our marriages. This challenge—in which even church leaders fall short—is what this book is aimed to help you accomplish. We want to help you build your marriage to resist storms.

One Key, Many Locks

Tim (as I will call him) is an elder and a Bible teacher in his church. He teaches Logos Bible courses and is highly respected in his congregation. Yet despite his familiarity with the Bible, he had not understood the pattern of Christ or its application to his marriage.

One day his wife Sally walked out on him and moved in with friends in a nearby city. She had been deeply embittered when, during a long illness, Tim had virtually ignored her, and rarely visited her in the hospital. This neglect had inflicted deep wounds, and when Sally expressed her hurt, he had merely defended himself, and had not apologized or expressed care. For five years she harbored this hurt, fuming about it from time to time as an offense that had never been healed. He euphemistically complained that she was gifted with "a good memory."

I told Tim about the principle of faith working through love and asked him to reflect on how he could practice this principle in his home life. When Sally moved back a couple of weeks later, he began by asking forgiveness for ignoring her. Tim's story is still being told, and we have not yet seen the conclusion. But it was amazing to see the light go on in him when he began to recognize the application of God's word in his home life. It is astonishing to see how blind we often are when it comes to the relationships that are closest to us, and how Jesus wants us to conduct those relationships.

Sins of Omission Are Hard to Identify

Paul and Virginia were stressed out from trying to maintain two jobs while raising a family. Paul ran a grocery store that occupied his days. Virginia was a police dispatcher who worked mostly at night. This day/night routine worked out well as far as child-rearing was concerned, but Paul and Virginia never took time to build their relationship with each other. They were so preoccupied with earning money and raising their two children that they ignored the pattern of faith working through love with each other.

The failure to follow the pattern of Christ left this couple ripe for a storm. One day Virginia didn't come home from her dispatch job. She had grown to feel that her marriage was empty and meaningless. Another man had come into the picture whose words and actions toward her did not seem so empty and meaningless, and she became romantically attracted to him. Fortunately, she did not commit adultery, which would have further complicated her marriage. Paul was shocked to realize how empty their marriage had become, and how little it meant to Virginia. The shock hit him like a ton of broken hearts. Paul (who was the first to come for help) and Virginia learned through counseling Christ's pattern of faith working through love. They had not realized that there is a marital pattern in Christ, thus opening themselves to a storm that almost blew their marriage away. As a result of counseling—by practicing faith working through love—they repaired their relationship and put it on a sound footing.

The Fix-It Mentality

We Americans don't like to adjust our pattern of living. When our teeth decay because we rarely brush them, we go to dentists with the hope that they will fix the problem without it costing us too much. We expect our dentist to fix the problem. After all, dentists are professional tooth fixers. They go to school for that very purpose. The teeth to be fixed may be our teeth, but we do not have a degree in how to fix them. One thing we know: the dentist's expertise is the solution to our tooth decay problem, and we are willing to pay whatever it takes to fix our teeth.

When the dentist tells us to brush and floss more regularly, we think, "Why do we have dentists? I don't want to have to brush and floss. It's too much trouble. Brushing and flossing defeats the purpose of dentists." It seems easier to wait until a regular torture trip (checkup) than to have to bother with changing our whole daily routine.

Prophylaxis

What Jesus is saying is the same as the dentist: "If you will hear my words and obey them, when the eventual tor-

ture trip comes, you will not be blown away with bad news."
Jesus believed in preventive medicine—prophylaxis, to use
a good dental term. He believed in building a pattern for living that would keep marriage from deteriorating in the first
place—as opposed to waiting until something goes wrong,
and then fixing it. Therefore, the principle of faith working
through love is not only good for healing what ails your marriage; it also helps prevent marriage decay.

Healing and Prevention

Wayne is struggling with his business. He comes home
after a particularly grueling day and says to his wife, Dede,
"Sometimes I feel like giving up. I wonder if it's worth it.
Three employees quit, and we lost a pile of money to
shoplifters." This is a confession of his need, an invitation
for her to support and encourage him.

If Dede were to respond by using the pattern of faith
working through love, they could stand together facing a
cold, cruel world and their problems would actually bind
them together more closely. They could spend the rest of
the evening ministering to each other in body, soul, and
spirit.

Instead, Dede bitterly says, "If you treated your employees with any care, you wouldn't be in this mess." Her words
hurt Wayne so deeply that Wayne reels with pain for five
days. The rebuke incapacitates him, not because it is untrue,
but because it reflects no love. Dede has not yet understood
how to speak the truth in love, a subject we will deal with
later.

Wayne and Dede are trapped in a vicious circle. They tear
each other down, and each new round of doubt working
through hate digs the circle deeper. We want for them not
only to be healed of immediate hurts, but also to learn a
new pattern so they won't keep hurting each other. Both of
them together must come to see how they are falling short

of Christ's pattern. Both together must change habitual ways of relating to each other.

Gimme a Pill, Doc

Doctors must get pretty tired of smokers and alcoholics who want medical attention for diseased lungs and livers. What can the doctor do? The "fix-it" mentality is completely out of touch with the reality of what these patients are doing to their bodies day by day. They keep choosing the wrong pattern, and pay for it in diseased lungs and livers.

The doctor tells them to stop drinking and smoking. To accomplish this they must invest in a program and learn a new pattern. A quick trip to the doc won't do it.

Jesus must often feel like those doctors. People hope for miracles from the great miracle worker. And, of course, sometimes he obliges us. But what Jesus gives us for most situations is a revealed pattern of living, faith working through love.

Question: Are you willing to look at how your lifestyle may contribute to an unhealthy marriage? Or do you think that making a good marriage should be effortless—like popping a prescribed pill? Are you prepared to look at your pattern of life and work for constructive changes?

Question: Looking at your own lifestyle (not your partner's), what are you doing that you already recognize to be unhealthy and destructive for your marriage? Make a list just for starters. Include not only things you do, but things you don't do.

Converting a Dam into a Dynamo

Withheld love, belittling words, and violation of our integrity drain us of energy. Hurts can incapacitate us until we have no energy to solve the problems of life.

Like Tim, who was described in the first part of this chapter, both Ev and I have discovered that when we withhold love from our wives, their stress level goes up. They need the security of our love. When they have it and know that they have it, they are bundles of energy for piano teaching, church ministry, prayer, writing, and mothering our children. But when we forget to do our part, they become stressed out. They lose confidence, become impatient. They become a bundle of nerves, not of energy. It is as though the flow of life becomes blocked. Something is dammed up in the psyche. Most men do not see the connection between their wives' behavior and their own lack of faith working through love.

In some homes, a dam made of problems has grown up to block the flow of life. It is a thousand-feet high and a hundred-feet thick. Yet the very problems that form this dam in the Valley of Trouble can be the material to build a dynamo. Some people build dams *because* they need energy, but a dam that merely holds back stagnant water gives no energy at all. The Valley of Trouble is an excellent location not only for a dam but also for a dynamo. We must learn how to put the dynamo into the dam. The dynamo is the pattern of Christ—faith working through love. There is power in the pattern of Christ.

I Found the Dynamo

When I stopped running away from the marital problems my wife was telling me about, when I began haltingly to love Carla enough to listen to her needs, and when I trusted God to give direction to my love, the marriage problems themselves drew us together and energized our love.

I had to have enough faith in God to face Carla when it looked like she could tear me down. In faith I had to decide to love her and to trust God to pick up the pieces if she

exploded at me. At times, I simply had to keep my eyes on
God while she was voicing her anger over a disappointment,
and try to show her that I cared how she felt. At times, she
has had to do the same thing when she failed to meet my
expectations—faith working through love.

It is after such times as these, allowing the relationship
to flow through the difficulty—instead of avoiding the difficulty—that Carla and I have enjoyed our most intimate
times in each other's arms. We found the truth of Paul's
words in Ephesians 5:13, that darkness exposed to the light
becomes light. The difficulty itself becomes the opportunity of love. The barrier becomes a hurdle. The Valley of
Trouble leads to the Pass of Hope.

The pattern of Christ enables us to find new energy to
deal with whatever problems we face.

"I Shouldn't Have Problems"

Many people think: I'm a Christian. I shouldn't have marriage problems. Yet it may be that Christ himself has brought
us into a Valley of Trouble because in his mercy he wants
to teach us his ways. Marital peace is not necessarily his
goal for us. We are the ones who want peace at all costs.
He wants to change our character, to make us more like
him. Marriage is one of his many tools to do this. Jesus sees
that, at times, without marital troubles, we remain petty,
self-centered, lustful, greedy, or fearful. He wants to roust
us out of our stagnant backwater and pour us into the Valley of Trouble.

Troubles are no fun, but they can be good for us. By them
we are challenged to obey the pattern of Christ. In the end,
we are better off for having learned to do that. But let's look
more closely at the pattern of Christ, just to make sure that
we comprehend it. We must examine the nature of Christian
love, as it differs from other popular ideas of love. Then we
must look at why faith is an important part of the equation.

3

Value

Jesus' shortest parable is dynamite.

> The kingdom of heaven is like a merchant in search of fine pearls, who, on finding one pearl of great value, went and sold all that he had and bought it (Matt. 13:45–46 RSV).

The shortness of this parable leaves much for us to guess at, but an examination of the other parables in Matthew 13 provides an important clue. In all the others, Jesus himself is the subject of the parable. He is a sower of seed, a planter of mustard seed, a woman baking bread, a fisherman, and a treasure hunter. So here, too, the merchant must be Jesus.

What, then, are the pearls? They are the people for whom Jesus died. He gave up everything to purchase us for himself. In the eyes of Jesus, we are pearls of great value.

But Jesus says that he found *one* pearl of great value. In this expression he is telling us that he values each of us individually. He doesn't look upon us as one among millions, but as one in a million. He doesn't save us in batches of thousands, but one by one. Jesus would have died for any of us, if we had been the only person on earth.

Behind the few words "he sold all that he had" is the interpretation Jesus gave to his own impending death. His death was a purchase, a barter. No one trades something valuable for something cheap. We trade something we own for something that is more valuable to us. If it weren't more valuable in our sight, we would say, "No deal." Jesus, by dying, was showing in what high esteem he holds us. He values us more than his own life.

"In this is love, not that we loved God, but that God loved us and gave up his Son for us." Jesus interprets love as value. Jesus treats us like a pearl of great value. Jesus showed us what love is. Then he said, "Value one another as I have valued you."

Energy

When we feel valuable, we have seemingly infinite energy. Nothing can get us down. We are unstoppable, unconquerable. We rise to great heights, whatever the challenge. We get up in the morning with the sense that we are kings and queens. Joy and peace fill our hearts, and we are ready for whatever comes.

When we are not valued, or when we are actually devalued, our energy is drained away. We feel insecure, always wanting to prove ourselves, yet doubtful that we can. We feel unsettled, fearful, and easily hurt over the most trivial matters. We seem to be a bundle of wounds. We feel that we have lost the energy to love.

What Is Hurt?

The need to have value, and to know that we have value, seems to reside at the core of each of us. We cannot ignore it. To destroy our value is to hurt us as deeply and as destructively as it is possible to do. We should therefore take stock of what creates such deep and lasting hurt that many people commit suicide or turn to drink and drugs to assuage the pain.

There are three ways to devalue a person. Most of us seem to instinctively understand these three ways even in preschool and elementary school: we can ignore a person; we can violate a person; we can belittle a person.

To be ignored is to be treated as though we have no importance, no significance. *To be violated* is to be robbed of our integrity, abused for someone else's power or pleasure. *To be belittled* is to be made small in the eyes of others.

To Be Ignored

Pete spends late hours at work. He loves his job. Now that his life is consumed by his vocational ambitions, he finds his wife rather unattractive. Even when he comes home in time for dinner, he takes the plate off the table (full of the dinner his wife lovingly fixed for him), goes into the living room, turns on the TV, plops into his favorite chair, and settles in for a ball game. He wants to relax. He places little value on his wife or her needs. Relaxation occupies his attention.

Pete's wife feels devalued because he is ignoring her—not just occasionally, but day after day. He would not, of course, say flat out that he doesn't love her. He believes that he does love her. Doesn't he share with her his hard-earned money? Yet by ignoring her, he devalues her. She feels hurt by his neglect. Since Pete hasn't "done anything to her," he can't sympathize with her hurt feelings when she complains about his TV ball games. All the same, he is failing to love her.

To Be Violated

Chad is an alcoholic. Deep within him he is struggling with the low self-worth that comes from having grown up with an alcoholic father. He responds to this sense of his own smallness by demanding absolute submission from his wife. He takes frequent opportunities to demand his "conjugal rights" from his wife, claiming that the Bible supports him in this. He also insists that his wife obey him even in unrighteous decisions—such as the occasional dishonest business scheme. "After all," he says, "I am the head of this household, and your job is to submit to my decisions and be my helpmate."

If Chad's wife, following her conscience, balks at slavish obedience to her husband, he flies into a rage, abusing his wife, slapping and cursing her. He uses his superior strength to force her to obey him. Both sexually and personally he is violating her, and thereby destroying her value. He believes that by lowering her value, he can build up his own. He feels the power of his superior physical strength, and he hoards the widow's mite of worth he can glean from lording it over his wife. He would dearly miss her if she left him—because such an act would utterly devalue him. But he does not understand the concept of valuing and energizing her as Jesus and the apostles command: "Build up one another in love."

To Be Belittled

Eric and Marcia are in a financial pit. Eric tries to discuss this with his wife. He suggests that they make a budget. Marcia is suspicious. She feels that much of the problem is Eric's selfish spending. She has often felt deprived of what she has wanted to buy for herself. Somehow, the money is always spent on computer gadgetry, never on the arts and crafts that Marcia enjoys as a hobby.

She responds to Eric with nonverbal sarcasm and skepticism. A thousand times before, Eric has seen derision flowing from her like a powerful torrent— the rolling eyes, the deep sigh of scorn that says, "Deliver me from this imbecile I have married." Without saying anything, Marcia makes Eric feel like crawling under the table.

Marcia would have tried to destroy whatever suggestion Eric might have made. She long ago stopped taking his suggestions seriously. Eric and Marcia are in a war that has lasted for years. Whenever Eric makes a positive step, Marcia gets more enjoyment from destroying him than from trying to solve their problems. Finally, Eric cries despairingly, "What's the use?" He drops the budget idea, which might have been a means of getting some control over their spending.

The budget problem is not the only problem they face. They also face a value deficit problem. They have run each other's value so low that both of them have overdrawn each other's accounts. Their value as persons is an underlying issue that will prevent them from resolving every other issue they face.

A WOUNDED WORKER CANNOT BUILD

A construction worker who breaks his leg can't climb the scaffold and resume his bricklaying. He must heal first. Then he can get back on the job. Finances are a part of our household life that we must build brick by brick, but when the two workers on the marriage site are wounded, they cannot build this or any other part of household life. How can Eric and Marcia gain financial solvency? They are both wounded workers. The more they wound each other, the less capable they are of solving their financial problems.

The Issue behind the Issues

There are many issues that rise up like porches and gables on the marital house we are building. The most common marital issues are

- Finances
- Children

- Chores
- Sex
- In-laws
- Vacations and Leisure Time

Each area needs up-building if our household is to become secure and productive.

Yet underneath these issues is an underlying one that usually affects all of the other issues. Do the two builders on the construction site upbuild each other in love? Or do they, like a Laurel and Hardy comedy, keep knocking each other's heads with boards, and inadvertently kicking each other in the groin?

Wounded workers cannot build. They may go to counseling, read books, listen to tapes and sermons, or talk to each other till the cows come home about sex, budgets, chores, and Christmas with the in-laws, but they cannot get anywhere. They cannot arrive at solutions. They cannot build. They must first learn to heal each other's destroyed value. They must learn to practice the pattern of Christ. Faith working through love.

Do you see how important the pattern of Christ is? Jesus was right: if we cannot learn to practice this pattern, our house cannot stand. The least storm of life will knock it down.

Marriage can be an environment where two people have learned to energize each other for the challenges of life. Marriage, after all, was God's idea. He revealed to us that we could be stronger by being married than by remaining single (though the Apostle Paul recommended singleness to those who are content with it and who have the gift of celibacy).

But if this mutual energizing is to take place, we have to get beyond natural patterns that we have learned during our younger years—where we devalue other people, or where we simply fail to value them.

Question: In what ways do you actively devalue, or fail to value your partner? Try to get beyond immediate conflicts and ask yourself: *Am I healing, valuing, and loving my partner in the way that he or she needs, to be energized for living?* Be sure to take stock of both areas: words and actions that fail to value (by ignoring), or that devalue (by belittling and violating).

4

Faith in Jesus

There are times when two people are so deeply absorbed in tearing each other down that they cannot escape from this pattern. One destructive word invites another and another in an unending chain of retaliation. They soon feel trapped in each other's presence, bound into each other's stranglehold by invisible weblike threads in which each is being eaten alive by the other.

Porn and Obesity

Charles is into pornography. For him porn is a deeply ingrained obsession and compulsion. Without realizing it, he is committing a sin against his wife, Sheila. At least this is the implication of what Jesus said, that "he is committing adultery in his heart." The "lust of the eyes" is a sin against one's wife and against women in general. Slowly, Charles' attitude toward Sheila changes as he compares her boyish physique with the tempting pictures in his *Hustler* magazine and skin flick videos. In fact, his attitude toward all women has changed the more he gives himself over to porn. He regards women as female bodies that have appeared in his life solely for the satisfaction of his sexual desires and power needs. He feels cheated for having a wife who is not as "good" as the fantasies that now fill his mind.

Sheila senses Charles' growing disdain for her. She feels devalued. Sex with her husband feels like violation. She doesn't want to be a third-rate pinup girl, a prostitute who just happens to be married to the man who uses her. She would like to boobytrap his *Hustlers* with gunpowder—as suggested in the film "Fried Green Tomatoes"—or burn them in the incinerator out back. Yet she is fearful to confront a habit so deeply ingrained in her husband's life.

She responds to the pain of low self-worth by eating more than she should, then vomiting it up. She is bulimic. Food is her consolation. Yet she is deeply depressed by low self-worth, which is fed and nurtured by Charles' addiction to porn. She retaliates by withholding sex and withdrawing from a meaningful relationship with Charles. She cannot forgive him for his sexual fantasies; she feels that he is vile and foul. As she grows more gaunt, he becomes more disgusted with her, and turns increasingly to pornography. He feels justified in doing so, too.

How can Charles and Sheila find a way out of the pit that they have dug for each other? Each devaluing act puts them deeper into enslaving habits that they find more and more unsatisfying.

Their marriage is dying.

Disrespect and Withdrawal

Don and Bonnie's boys are out of control. All three of them are hyperactive. Bonnie is a tiny woman who learned to compensate for her smallness with a loud and belligerent voice. Shouting is how she has learned to deal with her children, too. When the boys act up, she yells at them.

They, in turn, have learned to ignore her, for she never disciplines them, and they don't care whether she shouts at them or not. Although they don't enjoy her yelling, they joke about it behind her back, and the jokes make her yelling tolerable. Don is a quiet man, who wishes that Bonnie were not so loudmouthed. He feels, perhaps rightly, that his boys would respond better to firm discipline with less shouting, but he senses that his wife does not have confidence in his ability to be a strong male influence in his boys' lives. She always pre-empts him, like a bridge partner with a weak hand and a long suit, who takes the bid away from both her opponents and her partner.

Over the years Don has grown resentful of Bonnie's apparent lack of respect for him. But instead of speaking his heart openly and directly, he withdraws from her and the three boys in angry silence. He is frequently depressed. He senses his ineffectiveness as a father, yet is paralyzed from taking any action.

Bonnie responds to his inaction by shouting and cursing even more. She is becoming increasingly frustrated with Don because he spends so much time moping, lying in bed, and sitting at the bar in the Flamingo Room down the street, nursing his anger in frustrated silence.

Both Charles and Sheila, and Don and Bonnie are trapped in vicious circles. They are unable to break out of patterns of mutual devaluing that they have fallen into. They desperately need to be valued. Yet they continue to devalue each other without realizing it. Each devaluing act begets a like response from the spouse. As a result, they always feel drained, stressed, angry, and mistrustful of each other.

Question: What vicious circles can you identify in your marriage and family? In what ways do you feel trapped in habitual patterns of mutual devaluing? Don't just think of

ways your partner devalues you. Think about your own way
of perpetuating vicious circles.

Even where two people do not intend to devalue each
other, their insensitivity can ensnare them in the same
vicious circles as if they intended to devalue each other.
When spouses don't actively devalue each other, but fail to
value and love each other positively, the effect is still the
same. If they want to align their marriage with God's will,
they must recognize that the pattern they have chosen is
not the pattern of Christ. They must turn away from it and
seek to conform themselves to God's word.

It may take years before they recognize how far they are
from the pattern of Christ. What makes it difficult to do so
is lack of understanding, power, and trust.

Understanding

To gain understanding we need to accept the revelation
of Christ, that love means valuing others (as we have
described in the above chapters). Then we have to understand what behaviors will help others to feel like pearls of
great worth.

Power

In marriage we find out how elusive is the power to love
another person. Each partner has vowed to love the other
"until death do us part." Yet we soon become aware of
aspects of our partner's character that make him or her difficult to love. We can learn to accept little idiosyncracies—
peculiar ways of speaking, habits like wolfing down food,
or leaving the shower curtain outside the bathtub and the
toilet seat up. We can be patient about trivialities like that—
perhaps.

But other habits drive us up the wall. Our partner neglects, violates, or belittles us in ways that we find intolerable. Because we perceive these behaviors as an attack upon ourselves, we feel powerless to return love. As long as we receive love, we can give love. But a harsh word, a month of cold shoulders, or a single act of physical violence can turn love off like an electrical power failure. At such times we wonder how we could have ever loved our spouse. We think, "Was I insane to marry this person?"

We also may well ask, how can our love be restored? How can I love my partner after what he or she has done?

What Are the Power Options?

If Don gets his only self-worth from Bonnie, and Bonnie refuses to give it to him, Don is up the proverbial creek. If he chooses, he can look for self-worth elsewhere. Then he will have a source of self-worth that will empower him to love Bonnie whether or not she returns his love. Perhaps he can see that she feels unlovely, that she felt unlovely even before her wedding day. She needs to have someone in her life who will make her feel like a pearl of great price. Don can draw upon that other source for his self-worth, and then he will have love to give her to help her feel valued.

Jesus the Pearl Merchant

Now we return to the merchant in search of fine pearls. Jesus loves Don, but Don must have faith in that love, or it will do him no good. Jesus has done much for Don—died, been raised, ascended to a place of power, poured out the Holy Spirit, and established the Church as an environment where faith and love can grow. Don has to believe in these things, though, or they will never become a source of power or strength for his struggles at home.

Remember—the pattern of the Christian life is faith working through love. By faith, the apostle Paul means *faith in the power and love of Jesus the pearl merchant.* At first, Don may find that his faith is weak. The proclamation of what Jesus has done to purchase Don is only the faintest glimmer of strength in his life.

As he reads about Jesus' love, internalizes it, lets it into his imagination, and nurtures it by going to church, love grows. After a while, Don may see and truly feel that nothing can separate him from God's love (Rom. 8:35), that there is no condemnation for those who are in Christ Jesus (Rom. 8:1), and that God works all things together for the good of those who love him and are called according to his purpose (Rom. 8:28). The more he feeds on the love of God in Jesus, the more he feels the power of God's acceptance. He feels stronger than ever because he senses that he is valued by his Creator. Others at church love and value him, too. They are good at representing God to him, which makes it easier to believe in God's love. Faith has opened the floodgate in the dam of the Valley of Trouble. Soon he will feel the energy of God's dynamo.

Trust

With that energy flowing at the core of his being, Don can now turn toward his wife, who doesn't respect his manliness—or at least he thinks that she doesn't—and see that God is calling him into manliness. He might even see that his perception about Bonnie has been wrong all along. He is lifted above his former way of looking at his wife. When his boys misbehave and his wife yells, he does not need to retreat into the bedroom. He courageously deals with the misbehaving boys. His new source of strength and courage come from the self-worth that flows from Jesus into his life. His trust in God takes over, even when he distrusts his wife.

Don's ability to discipline his boys in love, and even to confess his sense of being belittled and disrespected by his wife, are directly related to his faith in God's love for him.

Faith is the anchor that ties him to the solid rock. Without a solid rock, his vicious circles were quagmires from which he could not lift himself. But now he has found solid ground in Jesus.

The pattern of the Christian life is not characterized by love alone. Love by itself works all right wherever love is not tested. But when love is tested, we must have something stronger to carry us through the test than mere good feelings or good intentions: faith working through love is the pattern of Christ. This love is anchored in faith and confidence that Jesus died for us, bartering his life to purchase us for God.

"Give Him to Me"

Kirby was becoming discouraged at my (Ev's) inability to show love and affection in a way that she could receive it. She became depressed as she reviewed her unmet expectations about our marriage. She tried to decide how she was going to get me to fill her needs better than I was doing. She wanted verbal expressions of love, but I could give her only hugs and encouraging pats. A dozen times already I had said that I would try harder. A dozen times I had failed.

She went to see our pastor. Through him God spoke to her. "Give Ev up to me. Give me your desires. Let me work on Ev in my way."

As a result of this challenge, Kirby trusted God with her frustrations. She was able to release her concerns about me, and she earnestly tried to give her deep needs to God. She began to focus more on how she could show love and affection toward me in ways I could receive it, rather than looking to me to fulfill her needs. She also developed friendships with other Navy wives that met some of her needs for intimacy. She believed that God had other ways of meeting her intimacy needs than through me alone.

This decision of faith helped both Kirby and me to relax. I was able to sense her acceptance. When she needed affection, she was able to show affection to me. She took initiative, rather than stewing about me. Her acceptance freed me to love her. I was not able to be all that my wife wanted me to be, but we had more peace between us and could learn a free and voluntary love for each other. This came from her willingness to look to God more deeply to meet her need to be valued. No human being can totally meet our need to be loved. God alone can fully meet that need.

Her decision affected our marriage. It gave me the freedom to keep growing as fast as I could, without the pressure of her immediate needs making me feel inadequate. Not only that, but her decision drew me directly to Jesus. I saw his love in her and I wanted it.

Simon the Pharisee

We see the pattern of faith working through love in a story by Luke the physician. Jesus was having dinner in the home of Simon the Pharisee. Into this prim and proper household barged a woman of the streets. No doubt she was dressed seductively, with thick makeup, and raven black hair cascading over her shoulders.

Such carnal people rarely found their way into Simon's house, and Simon was astonished that Jesus didn't discern what kind of woman this was. When she bowed before Jesus, wet his feet with her tears, and wiped them with her hair, Jesus let her do it. Simon's face fell. He condemned Jesus for the company he kept and for his lack of moral discernment.

Seeing the judgment in Simon's face, Jesus spoke:

Do you see this woman? I came into your house. You did not give me any water for my feet, but she wet my feet with her tears and wiped them with her hair. You did not give me a kiss, but this woman, from the time I entered, has not stopped kissing my feet. You did not put oil on my head, but she has poured perfume on my feet. Therefore, I tell you, her many sins have been forgiven—for she loved much. But he who has been forgiven little loves little (Luke 7:44–47).

This woman, though treated like a piece of gravel by society, had learned that she was a pearl of great price to Jesus. Her faith had produced a love that drove her to Christ. It surely wasn't easy for her to rush into the home of those who most despised her, and pour out her heart toward Jesus in their presence. But her faith in the love of Jesus, which she had gained before this story began, strengthened her to do what would otherwise have been impossible: to ignore those who despised her and to keep on loving despite their belittling scrutiny.

Jesus' words to Simon convey the connection between being loved and being able to love, between being forgiven and being able to forgive. We cannot give what we have not received. Jesus was saying that this woman had already received God's forgiveness, or she couldn't have poured out her love as she was doing.

We see here that, if we are to love our spouse, we will do a better job of it if we have received the love and forgiveness that Jesus offers us. Receiving God's love by faith is at the very center of the Christian pattern.

We must receive God's forgiveness and love by faith if we are to break out of our vicious circles. God's forgiveness and love become a new strength in which we can face the devaluing words and deeds of a partner who looks down his or her nose at us, who violates us, and who scorns us.

Question: Do you find it easy or difficult to believe that God loves you?

Question: In what situations do you need to remind yourself of the love of Jesus when you are around your spouse?
Are there times when your spouse habitually catches you
off guard at a weak moment, and you react unlovingly? How
would your remembrance of Christ's love for you change
your reaction?

5

Christianity

If faith working through love is the pattern of Christ, we must try to apply that pattern to our marriages. There are eight dimensions of marriage that bring either pain and emptiness, or fullness of life. These are

- Christianity
- Core Vision of Marriage
- Confession and Forgiveness
- Closeness, Intimacy
- Communication
- Conflict Management
- Cognition
- Covenant and Committment

This chapter deals with the first of these dimensions of marriage.

Christianity, the Source of the Pattern

Not everyone sees Christianity as a pattern for living. Some people see it as a religion. We must therefore begin this chapter with a definition of terms. Is Christianity a religion, or a way of life?

If we believe that Christianity is a religion, we will let it affect only the one corner of our mental house marked "religion." That small closet is where we keep God, carefully circumscribing his influence, trying to control God so that he doesn't get out of hand. As for the rest—vocation, vacation, hobbies, habits, vices, pleasures, hopes, *and marriage*—we assume that God has little to do with these parts of our living space. When we approach Christianity as a religion, we may carefully build our lives to prevent interference from God.

Consider Jesus. It was not his religiosity or piety that impressed people. He loved people and healed them. Who could possibly object to all the good works that he did?

Yet many people did object, and they tended to be the "religious" people of Israel. Jesus threatened to upset their carefully controlled and ordered lives. They couldn't handle Jesus walking freely outside the Temple, doing the works of God and calling people to *follow a pattern.* Feeling judged by a higher way of life, they killed him. Yet he refused to stay in the tomb-closet where they had dispensed with his body.

Could it be that religious people even today are unwittingly the enemies of Christ, not his friends?

Doug's Personal Surrender to Christ

About twenty years ago, after seminary, I discovered to my shame that I identified more with the religious professionals who put Jesus to death than with Jesus and his disciples. I wanted to call the shots in my life. I wanted to control God. I believed in "decency and order," and if God wouldn't fit into my ambitions, I had little use for him. I wasn't really sure whether he existed anyway—though I was a pastor of a church.

But I soon grew weary of the emptiness of my life as a religious professional, and I surrendered my life to God. I moved out of religiosity and into Christianity. I let God show me how to build my life according to his pattern. Among the areas of life that were affected by this decision was my marriage.

For instance, until that time, I had castigated my wife for her manipulative ways of getting me to express love to her. After my surrender to Christ, I realized that God himself wanted me to express love to my wife. I had to submit to God's will, the pattern of the Christian life for marriages. "Husbands ought to love their wives as their own bodies. He who loves his wife loves himself" (Eph. 5:28).

In light of my free decision to follow the pattern of Christ, I began not to react negatively to the things she said, but to carefully evaluate what she said by asking, "Is this of God?" When it came to loving my wife in expressive, cherishing ways, I had to admit, this was God's will.

This recognition broke us out of patterns of mutual manipulation. Both of us wanted to please God, so we had to submit to God's will. Not surprisingly, we found that God's ideas worked better than ours.

God Shouts to Us Through Marital Struggles

Jesus Christ can draw us to a place of deep surrender, in which we really try to listen to him, and submit ourselves to him. Often, marital struggles will bring us to the point where we see our need for him, and we are willing to judge ourselves according to his pattern, changing whatever does not fit his commandments.

Ev and I have known several people who were brought into a relationship with God because of their marital struggles. In such struggles, they saw the futility of trying to control the life of their spouse. They had been trying to make their spouse fall in line with their will. But changing a husband or a wife is as futile as turning Dracula into a fine Christian gentleman. They came to know the truth of Jesus' words, "Apart from me, you can do nothing" (John 15:5). In the face of marital troubles, they were drawn to their knees—where God drew them to learn how to trust him.

God's power to save, heal, and redeem a marriage requires of us a deep surrender, a deep trust in him. Jesus wants us to "abide in him and let his words abide in us" (John 15:7). He wants us to "take his yoke upon us and learn of him" (Matt. 11:29). If we want God to help us, we can't keep him in a religion-closet. We must let him teach us how to build a whole new life, trusting him day by day and asking him to give us the power to love our spouse with his love—regardless of how our spouse behaves.

From the vantagepoint of a surrendered life, marriage is no longer a struggle of two opposing wills. It is a mutual decision to please a third party—God. Each spouse gives up his or her self-will in a sincere decision to follow God and trust God to deal with his or her spouse. This new way of seeing each other and of dealing with our own willfulness can bring new hope to a shattered marriage.

Question: Could God be calling you to surrender your life more deeply to Jesus—regardless of any decision your partner makes in this regard?

Pseudo-Christianity

Often, when people begin to seek the pattern of Christ, the old ways continue to prevail for a time under the guise of Christianity. People still want to be in control, and it takes a while to reorganize their thinking, attitudes, and behavior, to let Jesus be in control.

They like to think that by subtle or not-so-subtle schemes, they can move their spouse to embrace Christianity. They leave books open on the coffee table, or strongly invite the spouse to church week after week. (The partner says they're nagging, but they know he or she is just hardhearted.) They press guilt buttons, complaining about their spouse's ungodly living and prayerlessness. Or they hold church meetings in their living room, hoping that the spouse will hang around and get pulled in.

What's the problem with these strategies? They're manipulative!

Jesus does not manipulate like that. He raised the cross in front of our faces and died for us, trusting that love itself would draw us to him. He did not say, "I will die for you—but promise me first that you will respond by following my ways." Jesus had no guarantees that anyone for whom he died would follow him. He trusted God to use his love as a powerful attraction to us. He followed the same pattern that he recommends to us: faith working through love. He rejected manipulative control masquerading as love. Still today, he gently shows us his ways, but lets us decide to follow him without pressuring us.

If this is Jesus' way, then it is also the way of a mature Christian, for the mature Christian is one who patterns his or her life after Jesus. Our spouses will not be converted to Christ through our cleverness in planting subliminal messages. They may be converted, slowly over time, by our willingness to be fountains of self-giving love.

When I (Everett) married, I was not a Christian. Though Kirby was a strongly committed Christian, God had miraculously blinded her to the "unequally yoked" verse in 2 Corinthians 6:14. Over the first few months of our marriage, though, it became obvious to me that Kirby had something

I wanted and needed—a spiritual vibrancy. Yet I was stubborn. I argued and resisted the way of Christ. Eventually, Kirby became frustrated and went to counseling with her pastor. He empathized with her and counseled her to stop arguing with me and merely to love and accept me. Within a couple of months, her loving character, and my knowledge of where her strength came from, had melted me. I began to grow in faith and to trust in Jesus. Paradoxically, Kirby's efforts to persuade me to be a Christian failed, but her persistent practice of faith working through love succeeded in drawing me to Christ.

Pseudo-Christianity may be manifested in a variety of ways. In many of these ways a Christian can get in the way of what God wants to do. For example, we get in the way when we:

- use Christianity to support our opinions or to get our way
- use the Bible as our own sword to hack at people, rather than as the sword of the Spirit of God to cut away our own sin
- nitpick about trivial concerns, while avoiding the love commandment
- take an attitude of spiritual superiority toward a partner, rather than encouraging the partner to take steps toward God
- enforce a list of harsh rules on spouse and children
- give only nominal assent to Christ—and thus teach by our example that Christianity is unimportant
- use our position as "head of the wife" to lord it over our wives, or use our position as "submissive wife" to avoid communicating honestly and openly with our partner

Question: Are there areas in which your Christianity has been subtly selfish or manipulative? Search the above list and see if any of these pseudo-Christian patterns might apply to you. What would it mean, in these areas, to "take up your cross and follow Jesus?" Is God prompting you to ask forgiveness for any unloving ways that you have portrayed Christ to your partner?

6

Core Vision of Marriage

One of the commonest complaints that comes out of a troubled marriage is that the marriage is empty. To a spouse who complains of this, the emptiness is as obvious as the Grand Canyon. Yet when he or she expresses this to the partner, the spouse finds the partner oblivious to the obvious. That the partner doesn't also feel the emptiness of the marriage suggests that the partner is not only obtuse but blind. The situation seems more than empty. It seems hopeless.

Yet the perception of emptiness is caused not so much by the obtuseness of one's spouse as by one's own expectations for marriage. What do you expect marriage to be *filled with?* What do you imagine to be the necessary core, the heart, the vitals of a good marriage?

For example, if you were of Abraham and Sarah's generation, the core of a good marriage would be children, preferably male. "An empty marriage is a childless marriage, a marriage of barren wombs and little girls," Sarah might

have said, wondering why anyone would even question
such an obvious premise.

Most Americans would not say that boy babies make a
marriage worthwhile. Our core vision is completely different from what Hebrew culture might have recommended.
Emptiness or fullness is relative. It is a matter of perspective, culture, and training. What may seem obvious to you
may not be obvious to your partner, because your partner
holds a different core vision of marriage, which yields different hopes and dreams. Your partner has a different perception of emptiness and fullness.

> **Question:** What do you believe to be so essential to a good
> marriage that a marriage is emptied of all meaning without
> it? What two or three ingredients should fill the core of a
> satisfying marriage?

Career versus Intimacy

Rob sees his marriage as a base from which he can
accomplish professional challenges. He sees his wife as a
helpmate that God has provided. He wants to enter the pastoral ministry, so he is attending seminary.

During their first year at seminary, Rob's wife, Bobbi, sacrifices for him. To earn his tuition, she holds a mundane job
stapling publications in a print shop. Bobbi's accommo-
dating decision fits to a tee Rob's picture of a good marriage. He feels that he has a full marriage because his core
vision is satisfied by his helpmate.

During the first two years of seminary, however, Bobbi
feels that her job at the stapling machine is boring. She
might tolerate it better if Rob were sensitive to her core
vision of marriage. To her, a good marriage consists of intimate talks, cherishing love, and the romance and sexual
closeness that grow out of that intimacy and love.

If Rob could see her core vision of marriage and build her up in it, all would be well. But he can't, and Bobbi doesn't realize that she must communicate her vision to her husband. She assumes that her core vision is *THE* core vision, and that everyone should have the same understanding of what is important in marriage as she does. She communicates nothing of her feelings, but grows increasingly dissatisfied with the emptiness of her life and marriage. She wonders, "How can I spend the rest of my life like this?"

As the semester nears the end, Rob spends more time at the seminary library than ever. His seminary prides itself in being a first-class intellectual institution, and Rob often feels challenged beyond his abilities. His one goal in life is to graduate with a decent grade point average. He thanks God for his wife, who, he assumes, wants him to graduate with flying colors, too. He believes that her core vision for marriage is the same as his, and that she is content to staple brochures.

The intellectual hoops that seminary requires Rob to jump through leave little time for Rob and Bobbi to spend on dates, in personal conversation, in romance, and lovemaking. Sex becomes a hurried encounter between textbooks, which repulses Bobbi. There might be time for true intimacy if Rob were willing to find it and if Bobbi could communicate her need. But in her silence Bobbi becomes more angry and bitter with each staple she punches. Each staple stabs one more hole in her self-esteem.

Finally, Rob's world crashes down around him when he returns to their apartment one day to find a " Dear John" note from Bobbi. She left Rob because her life with him was empty and unfulfilling. The emptiness of their marriage had made her job sacrifices worthless to her. To Rob, she seemed unwilling even to talk about trying to make the marriage work.

What went wrong? Both Rob and Bobbi were Christians. But Rob was so busy trying to excel in seminary that he forgot to put into practice biblical faith working through love. In the eyes of his professors, Christianity had become a question of how well one thinks, rather than how well one lives. Rob may have learned many interesting points about theology and biblical languages, but he did not learn how to apply at home the basic pattern of Christ. Seminary ambitions soon became a temptation to disobey the most basic word of God for all husbands: "Husbands love your wives as Christ loved the Church" (Eph. 5:25).

Bobbi's shortcoming was her failure to communicate her heart to her husband. She assumed that what she felt so strongly would be obvious to Rob. The failure of their marriage represented, on the one hand, a wrong perception of Christianity, and on the other, a failure to discuss their respective core visions of marriage.

Relationships and Challenges

Gary Smalley, the well-known marriage counselor and teacher, has pinpointed in his marriage seminars a common pattern that I (Doug) have seen not only in my own marriage but also in counseling other couples. One partner, usually the husband, is living his life for challenges. Challenges get him out of bed in the morning and occupy his mind all day. He (or sometimes she) sees the wedding day as a challenge that has been successfully completed. He looks forward to the next challenges, perhaps building a business, establishing himself in a profession, or changing the world into a better place.

The other partner lives for relationships, and sees marriage as the ultimate in relationships. She (or perhaps he) sees the wedding day as the beginning of a growing intimacy sealed by the wedding vows, to be nurtured until the partners are separated by death.

These core visions are different, and the differences between them can plant a seed of disillusionment from the first day of the honeymoon.

It took me many years to perceive this difference between my wife and myself. As I have already described, I was so caught up in my career that I could not see my wife's core vision of marriage as an intimate relationship. I am wired differently than Carla.

I remember going to a Marriage Encounter weekend about fifteen years ago. Carla had heard that these weekends were devoted to intensive husband-wife communication—the writing of love letters. This concept ministered to her core vision of marriage and she was excited. I went because I thought that I might pick up a few useful pointers in my counseling with couples. A Marriage Encounter weekend was a good way to advance my challenging career as a pastor and counselor.

I just didn't get it. Relationships were my short suit, and I had not yet learned to value my wife's long suit. I saw only my own hand and, like an inexperienced bridge player, I foolishly squandered my wife's good cards. How different my early years of marriage might have been if I had seen the value of the intimate relationship that she so highly prized. I wish now that I had let her core vision of marriage influence mine.

An Incomplete Core Vision

A core vision isn't static. Our core vision can change and mature. We can incorporate our partner's core vision into our own, so that the two are fused together. What is partial can become complete. If we communicate our dreams and hopes to each other lovingly and without condemnation, and if we are willing to bear patiently with a partner who is coming from a different place than we are, then we can both end up with a better marriage than if we simply pressed for our own idea of what marriage should be. We men are incomplete without our wives, just as our wives are incomplete without us. We have greater potential together than we would have walking separately through life.

In Charles Dickens' story, *A Christmas Carol*, Ebenezer Scrooge develops early in life a relationship with a young woman that is quickly moving toward marriage. However, Scrooge does not appreciate that his vision (owning a profitable business) is incomplete. He wants a wife who will support him in the challenge of developing his business, but he does not see the value of nurturing his relationship with her, of cherishing her, or investing time, money, and energy in building romance. He repeatedly stands her up because business meetings take precedence in his life over everything else, including his fiancee. He loves his business more than he loves her, though he would not express it that way.

Thus he commits the greatest sin of omission that a man can commit against his wife. He neglects her. She, of course, senses the lack of love, his devaluing of her. She finally breaks off the engagement, telling him that the breakup will hurt him but for a moment, and afterward he will be free to pursue his one true love—money—with greater abandon.

Ebenezer is flabbergasted by this rejection and cannot understand it. He does not appreciate that his core vision for life and marriage is incomplete. He had been telling himself that his pursuit of money was to provide a secure future for the both of them. He had thought that she had the identical idea.

Because Ebenezer could not see that his fiancee's core vision complemented and completed his own, he made no attempt to win her back or to prove his love. To admit that his instincts about life were incomplete would have wounded his pride. Instead, he drowned his brief sorrow in a flurry of business activities, pursued his partial vision with full devotion, and ended up a half-formed man with a shrivelled soul. He needed a woman to make a real man of him.

Could it be that God brings a person of the opposite sex into our lives because he wants to broaden our narrow vision of what life can be? A husband and wife who combine their visions of marriage are much more likely to attain God's complete vision. Perhaps that is the truth hidden behind the words that "in the image of God he created him; male and female he created them" (Gen. 1:27). The stature and fullness of Christ is to be found in the male and the female working harmoniously together.

My wife has helped me in this way—helped me to see the importance of a cherishing love, a type of love I saw no need for as a young man. Her core vision for marriage challenged my own, and I had to open my life to it, as she did to mine.

Ingredients of a Core Vision

We have mentioned only a few examples of how differing visions can stress out or bring happiness to marriage. Many other ingredients may enter into a core vision for marriage. In each, persistent, loving communication is needed to move beyond the emptiness of unmet expectations. We must say what is in our hearts, and we must listen to what our partner says, too. As we do, a new world of possibilities may open up. These possibilities may seem threatening at first, but will eventually become welcome and friendly as we see God's larger, hidden purposes revealed through our spouse.

Consider the ingredients of your core vision of marriage insofar as they include such elements as economics, romantic love, ministry, children, sex, companionship, and a secure home.

Question: Do you sense a difference between you and your spouse in your core vision for marriage? After giving plenty of time to describe the elements of your own core vision, talk about the differences between the two visions. What can you gain from incorporating your spouse's vision into your own? How can your spouse's vision enrich your own?

7

Confession and Forgiveness

A wounded worker cannot build. Woundedness interferes with our ability to work on our home life. If we are to keep our marriages alive, we must find ways to heal the hurts. We must learn what produces healing so that we may give energy to each other, rather than draining it from each other by the wounds we inflict.

"Confess . . . That You May Be Healed."

James, the brother of Jesus, correctly discerned how to heal relationships: "Confess your sins to each other and pray for each other so that you may be healed" (James 5:16).

The Apostle John wrote, "If we claim to be without sin, we deceive ourselves and the truth is not in us. If we confess our sins, he is faithful and just and will forgive us our sins and purify us from all unrighteousness. If we claim we have not sinned, we make him out to be a liar and his word has no place in our lives" (1 John 1:8–10).

There is nothing so galling to our spouse's sense of value as the conviction that we don't care that he or she is hurting. When we refuse to acknowledge our insensitivity or mistakes, our partner may interpret that as a lack of care—which often does more damage to a marriage than the original hurt. Often our partner will interpret a lack of confession as a lack of love—even though we may not have intended it as such. From the partner's point of view, this apparent lack of care inflicts wound upon wound—not only stabbing, but turning the knife.

Marriages Sick unto Death

In sick marriages, partners have wounded each other repeatedly without regret. Excruciating pain hides beneath a crusty exterior of scabs and scars. Neither partner is willing to do what heals. They enter counseling covered with bleeding wounds of the soul because they have violated each other, belittled each other, and ignored each other. Both defend themselves. They insist that their own hurtful actions are the inevitable response to the other's barbarities. How can they break out of their vicious circles?

Neither has exercised the faith that tries the pattern of Christ. Each plays the helpless victim who can only retaliate against the other's cruelties. Caught on a treadmill of harm, pain, and self-defense, they act as though Jesus had never died, had never commanded obedience, had never loved them with his empowering, inspiring love.

It comes down to this: a person of faith admits his or her mistakes; a person of little faith refuses to do so. True faith in Christ produces love. True love admits mistakes rather than defending them. To confess mistakes empowers one's partner. It says: "You are important to me. I am willing to humble my pride for you. I want you to stop hurting." Sincere confession is a way of loving, a way of valuing.

When No One Is Willing to Be Vulnerable

What is the alternative? To blame. To look good in the
eyes of the counselor. To win arguments. To play the game
of "Look how right I've been." Without seasons of vulner-
ability and confession, there is no healing. Hurts accumu-
late. Like impurities in the bloodstream, they poison everything. We may try to ignore our hurts, but the first devaluing
word will irritate hidden emotional boils. Anger resides just
beneath the surface, breaking out unexpectedly. On some
days, we are hypersensitive. On others, depression saps our
energy. We can scarcely drag ourselves from bed. At other
times, we suffer from sleeplessness because we are stewing about hurts. Our energy level plummets, for we are using
all our energy to fight emotional poisons within.

It is astonishing! A simple word of confession can save
a family thousands of dollars in medical and psychiatric
bills. But who will be the first to offer it?

Question: When you sense that your spouse has something against you, what prevents you from following
Christ's explicit instructions: "If your brother sins against
you, go and show him his fault, just between the two of
you" (Matt. 18:15)? Can you overcome these barriers, to be
set free, or to set your partner free from bitterness and
resentment?

Ev and I have seen couples spend hours in counseling
sessions trying to justify themselves against each other and
blaming each other for their blasted marriage. Then we ask
them to pray together that God might heal them. In prayer
they are melted before God. They easily confess their own
personal hardness of heart to God, which they could not
confess to each other during counseling. Unexpectedly, in
confessing sin to God, relational healing begins. Within five
minutes, their attitudes have changed. The hardness has

melted. They can leave counseling refreshed and energized. We have seen this phenomenon many times.

It wasn't necessarily our counseling that helped them. They simply did what Christ and the apostles recommended. The Holy Spirit was the counselor, giving scriptural balm for relational wounds. By obediently practicing the simple remedies of Christ, they saved themselves much pain and hours of unprofitable argument.

To Confess Is to Die

Why is confession so hard to do? Confessing one's faults is scary and difficult—because by it we die to self.

Soon after Carla and I arrived in Richmond, I noticed that she was closing off toward me. This, I have learned, is a sign that something is wrong between us. I have never violated my wife, never knowingly belittled her. But neglect is my middle name. I can easily become so involved in ministry, writing, and hobbies that Carla soon feels like a war bride.

Sensing that I had committed this sin for (at least) the 136th time, I arranged a lunch date with her at a nearby park. After our picnic lunch, I said, "Something has come between us. You've become distant. What's wrong?"

For me this is always scary—laying myself open to criticism, finding out about my inadequacies. Deep down, I fear that she'll hurt me. There were times when Carla might have laid into me. I had to risk that she might do it again. I was on a death-to-self picnic.

Yet I remembered how Jesus said that if I didn't die to myself, I wasn't worthy of him. So I went cheerfully to this picnic and practically asked my wife to kill me—with gentleness, I hoped.

She expressed how tired she was of feeling ignored, as though she were a household slave and not my wife. She remembered how, when I had courted her, I had written her poetry, had created ingenious ways to invite her to the movies, had conversed with her half the night. Now our marriage had become a hohumdrum nonaffair.

Hearing her complaints, I had to stifle the urge to defend myself, to make myself seem to have good motives for the ways I had failed her. "Why is it," I complained to myself, "that I am always the one with egg on my face? Can't I think of anything she has done wrong, just to balance the scales? And why, every six months, do I have to be confronted about the same thing over and over?" I was getting tired of this.

"Down, doggie, down," I commanded my own carnal nature. My goal, I remembered, was to restore my wife, to make her feel like a queen again. Defending myself wouldn't accomplish that. Besides, I wanted to be worthy of Jesus.

"I have become absorbed in my work," I admitted. " I've gone back into the absent-minded pattern that I've practiced before. I'm sorry. I've blown it again." I swallowed the last cookie and put my arm around her.

She knew I was listening to her and that I cared for her. The devaluing of six months of neglect was swept away in a moment of confession. Confession was the antidote to the poisons that had crept into our marriage.

Of course, this confession cost me. It was the cost to my vanity and pride that communicated value to her self-worth. Without cost there is no true valuing and little love. Cheap words convey little value. Costly words energize our partners and heal marriages. My words that day were costly.

We both knew that I would probably fail again, but that was not as important as reassuring her that I cared about her feelings and sincerely wanted to make our relationship right again.

At the end of our picnic, we talked about "solutions." We agreed to try to clear Friday nights for dates. (A date with my wife was an enjoyable prospect. I couldn't imagine why I was so reluctant to think of it or act on it.) She also asked me to acknowledge her when I came home in the evenings—even if it meant interrupting her piano teaching. My simple greeting was as important to her as was my kiss when we parted each morning. I learned again what my wife needed to keep our love alive, and her energy flowing. I admitted that I too needed that torch to burn more brightly, but it was Carla who saw more clearly when it was burning low, and who knew how to rekindle it. By confessing my lack of insight and sensitivity, I said to her, "Tell me what we need. Let me learn from you." This too conveyed value. I honored her insights. Confession provided healing. The practical suggestions that came second would have gotten us nowhere without the listening and confession that came first. Again, confession communicates value. Love is a willingness to value. Love heals and energizes.

(p.s.: What passionate love-making can sometimes follow such relational healing! But without such healing, sex is an empty giftbox.)

Question: How many times in your marriage have you spoken the words, "I'm sorry. Could you forgive me?" Is there perhaps a connection between times of health or sickness in your marriage and the frequency or infrequency of these words?

What Do You Do When There Is No Confession?

In situations of psychological distress and addiction, we sometimes have to endure long-lasting patterns of hurt, for which our partner has offered no confession or expressed any sorrow.

It is possible for a spouse, strengthened by faith in God, to love his or her partner into healing from addictive patterns. In such situations, a Christian can maintain a loving attitude that is largely one-way. For those who are married to dysfunctional people, love may require unilateral for-giveness—forgiveness that has not been asked for through confession of sin.

Unilateral forgiveness is a uniquely Christian option. Jesus models it, and beckons us to do likewise. Our Savior grants forgiveness unilaterally. There is no recorded instance in which anyone asked him to forgive them. It would seem that very few people confessed their sins to him—including those who persecuted him and who nailed him to the cross. Yet he forgave them and he prayed for them. By faith, Jesus obtained from the Father the power to forgive those who tried to destroy him.

In this he paved a way that he wanted us to follow and to imitate. "Forgive as the Lord forgave you" (Col. 3:13). Unilateral forgiveness is implied in the words, "Love your enemies and pray for those who persecute you" (Matt. 5:44). Jesus did not say, "pray for those who ask your forgiveness."

Normally, we forgive people only when they confess their faults to us. The idea of forgiving a person who has not con-fessed his or her faults may seem preposterous or beyond human ability. But in some situations, unilateral forgive-ness is the only hope for healing spouses and marriages. Addictive behavior may be such a situation. The addicted person may offer no confession for repeated hurts, or the confessions may seem less sincere with each passing year. Often, addicted persons themselves lose faith that they will ever change. Faith in Jesus Christ enables us to forgive uni-laterally in such situations, so that we are not eaten away by bitterness.

If we are to forgive and pray for a spouse who hurts us over and over, we need a source of strength that goes beyond human resources. By resting our self-esteem on the love of Jesus, we can be freed from the codependent manip-ulations that make addictive households so chaotic. By keeping our eyes on Jesus, we can avoid the pitfalls of bit-terness, the cover-ups, and the manipulations. We can practice tough love, godly confrontation, and risky truth-telling—for God wants us to speak the truth in love, not to confess sins we haven't committed or to pretend that we haven't been hurt when we have.

But in the midst of such truth-telling, Jesus can give us compassion for those who are trapped in dysfunctional patterns and who lash out against family members. We don't say that it is easy to love and forgive such people from the heart, but it is possible—through Christ alone. Christ can make us compassionate healers in the lives of deeply troubled spouses.

It can be a freeing insight to realize that God may call us to bring healing to a partner whose hurts go back to a childhood we had nothing to do with. This challenge requires us to depend on the resources of God more than we have ever done before. It is a high calling, and a humanly impossible one. But God has often called his people into humanly impossible callings, and showed them that he can work his miracles in seemingly hopeless situations.

Question: Are there any ways your partner has hurt you, when you remember no confession of faults to begin the healing process?

Question: Is it possible for you to get the ball rolling, not by taking full blame for those hurts, but by confessing the parts that were yours? Are you willing to do this, just because it is the right thing to do (it pleases God), regardless of the response of your partner?

8

Closeness

One of the most frequent sources of tension in marriage is caused by the pursuer-distancer problem. One partner feels the longing for a deeper marital intimacy. The other is quite happy with the status quo and can't understand or sympathize with those longings. The first spouse—usually the wife—pursues a closer relationship, while the other runs from it into job, hobbies, favorite TV sports, boyhood buddies, and so on.

We have already said that many women have a deeper sensitivity toward relationships than men and that many men relate more readily to challenges and feel out of their depth in the complexities of relationships. Women seem to have a natural expertise about what it would take to keep a marital relationship alive. (That is why most of the marriage and family books in the church library are checked out by women, not men.) One logical conclusion of this line of thinking is that husbands should listen to their wives' desires and grow more intimate with them.

Distance Is a Valid Need

Yet there is another side to this picture. Neither partner would be happy if both became totally fastened to each other—like Siamese twins joined at the hip and completely inseparable. If that were such an enviable lot, there would be no need for surgery to separate Siamese twins.

Most people do not really want to be completely inseparable from another person, to share everything and to have no separate life of their own. They would regard this as an intolerable intrusion, a hell on earth.

"I need my space," I heard a young woman say to an amorous boy named Benny, who was getting a little too affectionate. He was like a big puppy dog, always panting for intimacy with women. He never could understand that the young women whose psychological space he invaded had their own integrity and did not necessarily want to get into a heavy ultrapersonal conversation with him. Repeatedly women told him—some nicely, others rudely—"Give me space."

Other women's space has been violated more tragically by date rape or acquaintance rape. One such experience may be enough to make them chronically cautious and guarded around men. They understand the need for space.

Our point is that the intimacy issue is not always solved merely by men becoming more intimate with their wives. Space is important, too—important for both husbands and wives. Intimacy plus space equals love. It is a question of finding the right balance between the two, a balance that both partners are comfortable with. We must begin to sense when to be more intimate and when to allow more space. This is a fine art—painting our marriage canvas with proper amounts of intimacy and distance. Intimacy alone would make a monotonous work of art.

Question: Is there a "pursuer-distancer" problem in your relationship, in which one partner almost always requires more intimacy, and the other needs more space? If you are usually the pursuer, think of times when you were on the other side of the table, needing more space. If you are usually the distancer, remember times when you wanted more intimacy. Identify with your spouse's need; imagine where your spouse is coming from.

The Love Principle

The key to solving this problem is to understand the love principle and to practice it in this area. If both partners try to take what they need from the other, neither will end up with what he or she needs. If each is determined to give, to minister to the other's needs, both will end up satisfied.

This principle requires a shift from our usual orientation. Instead of trying to extract from the other what we require to feel fulfilled, we try to give the other what the other is trying to extract from us, while also communicating our own need. The distancing husband may plan times of intimacy with his wife; the pursuing wife may plan times to respect her husband's space (or vice versa, as the case may be).

Vacations

One occasion when the pursuer-distancer issue frequently comes up is during vacations. This past summer, Carla and I vacationed at a cabin high above the Potomac River to celebrate our 25th wedding anniversary. When I first proposed this way of celebrating our silver anniversary, Carla wasn't thrilled.

"You'll spend the whole time going on hikes and writing books," she said. She imagined that I was going to do what I have sometimes done on vacations—ignore her. Do my own thing.

For many women, vacations are the low point of the year. These times of retreat hold much potential for them because they and their husbands are away from the usual distractions of the office and the TV set. They imagine a time of intimacy and marriage renewal, memory-making conversations and shared explorations in God's world. Instead, their husbands go fishing, without even asking them to come along.

I have not been married for 25 years for nothing. I have learned some lessons about my wife. I have learned that if I give her what she wants (and what is good for both of us), she will give me what I want—space for writing and thinking. So we have developed a mutual giving relationship out of what used to be a mutual taking and manipulating relationship. This transformation is probably the main reason why our marriage has lasted 25 years.

I used to lecture her about how I needed space. Now I love her by attending to her need for more intimacy. I have found her a happier woman, one who meets my needs and is perfectly happy for my writing career and my hobbies. When she needs me to be more intimate and less distant, I make sure that I listen to her.

In planning our vacation, we agreed how we would spend some of our time. We took stacks of love letters we had written to each other during our engagement, and slides of the first years of our married life, which we hadn't viewed for twenty years because our children don't appear in them (and therefore they are not interested in seeing them). We spent the evenings reminiscing about our marital beginnings, and I made sure that we drew close together and spent much time together. In the mornings, after prayer, she was more than willing to respect the space I needed to write, while she read the Christian novels she loves so well. We didn't have to be Siamese twins joined at the hip.

On the other hand, Kirby and I (Ev) had a different type of vacation—three one-week camping trips to the Smokies and the Appalachians. Because our four children (ages 16, 14, 12, and 9) are running every which way most of the time, vacations are an important time of family togetherness. We hike together and talk, talk, talk. We tent camp and share adventures. (Someone once remarked that adventures are misery recollected in tranquility.) This year we had an "adventure" for a week in the Shenandoahs during a cold spell. We had left all sweatshirts and jackets at home—that gave us plenty to talk about while our teeth chattered. Intimacy.

Life is like dancing. Kirby and I enjoy ballroom and country-and-Western dancing together (Yee-haw, buckaroo). There are times of holding close, times of being at arm's length, and times of doing our own thing. For us, vacations, walks around the block, hiking in the mountains and parks, backpacking, picnics at the office, dancing, and making love are times of enjoyable togetherness. Those times sustain and energize us for the times at arm's length and times of individuality. Like Doug and Carla (only different), we have established a balance that's right for us.

The "Little Blessing" Has Arrived

Many of us have started our marriages with an engagement and honeymoon that were full of intimacy. Yet somewhere along the way the intimacy diminished and our marriages became more businesslike, mechanical, and uninspiring. Wives may tell their husbands that all the love has gone from the relationship. And if we are Christians, following the pattern of Christ, that should concern us.

For many couples, the transition from romantics to robotics happens when their first child is born. Few things unsettle marital equilibrium more than the arrival of a baby.

Never do three people seem so much like a crowd than when the three are husband, wife, and their first child.

Betty Sue—still sore from giving birth (they had to stitch her up)—sinks into a swamp of postnatal depression, a deflated feeling that matches what is happening to her tummy. She is both enthralled with and somewhat nervous about the responsibility of caring for this tiny infant, who is so helpless and dependent on her.

To her husband Joe, she seems preoccupied and distracted as never before. Joe is a little jealous of this intruder from within. This babe seems to be a spy, a mole working to sabotage the marriage from the inside. Though Joe is proud of the baby, he can scarcely bring himself to admit to the feelings of jealousy that have crept into his now triangular relationship.

Betty Sue's breasts, which he had enjoyed in his intimate moments with her, now at times belong to another. He must recognize that his wife's body was designed as much for nurturing babies as for his pleasure. His wife must be sensitive now to the needs of two people, not one. She must learn to love two people with one body—a new challenge not easily accomplished to everyone's satisfaction.

Stay in Touch

Sooner or later, most couples' intimacy is disturbed by the intrusion of circumstances—if not childbirth, then perhaps extended military service, a temporary night job, a career as an interstate truck driver, or aged parents moving into their household. These intrusions are not usually anybody's fault. Nonetheless they challenge the intimacy of husband and wife.

A couple can adapt to these changes only if they keep communicating with each other. In the case of childbirth, a husband can express his sense of being replaced by the baby. "At times, darling, I almost feel as though I've been replaced. Maybe it's jealousy, but I feel as though I've lost first place in your affections." He speaks the truth in love. She, in turn, can explain that her body hurts, that she couldn't dream of making love, but it isn't because she doesn't want to. She feels like a New England maple tree—draining liquids from every orifice. She hopes that he will be patient. She can use those massive hours when newborns sleep to show affection to her husband, while also asking him to be tender with her.

Neither partner assumes the worst about the other, but each builds on the intimacy they had at the beginning, expressing how valuable that was, refusing to let it slip away. Neither partner blames the other for allowing the child to remove romance from their marriage, but each tries to adapt to new realities, taking stolen moments to build on the intimacy that filled their marriage at the start.

God has designed in us a way of keeping alive our fascination for one another over the years. True, there is much that can go wrong with a couple's sex life, more than we could address in these few pages. Yet couples who have frequent sexual intercourse usually have a more vibrant marriage than those who do not. Couples who have vibrant marriages usually *want* to have sexual intercourse frequently.

Martin Luther, the Augustinian monk so influential during the Reformation, wondered why sexual incontinence, homosexuality, and unchastity were running rampant in the monasteries. As he read the Apostle Paul, he discovered that, according to the plan of God, most men were not gifted (as Paul was) to be celibate. The monks, including Luther himself, were going against their own God-created nature by holding up a false ideal of celibate sexuality. For the rest of his life, Luther made a practice of joining monks and nuns in wedlock. He married a nun himself, one of the most celebrated marriages in European history. Luther discovered that sex was designed for marriage. Marriage converted it from a curse to a blessing.

Have you ever wondered why God made sex such a powerful urge in human nature? Sex causes so many problems, especially in our culture, where we claim the right to have sex whenever, however, and with whomever we want. It causes disease, transmits the HIV virus, creates emotional pain, and invites guilt. With that potential for causing human suffering, why did God make it such a powerful and basic impulse?

He created it for marriage. Sex is a power for renewal of a relationship—if we are willing to allow it to be.

Here again it is the women who usually have the deeper sensitivity in relationships. Most men seem not to automatically connect sex with intimacy. Most women do. When women have extramarital sex, they usually feel that they have cheapened something that was meant to be sacred. If their partners spurn them afterwards, it is the women who seem to deal more intensely with the deep pain of tearing apart what has been "one flesh." Women, in short, seem to have a deeper awareness of what God says about sexual fidelity than do men, and when God's word is violated, it is women who feel God's pain more keenly.

"Talk to Me"

For that same reason, women must be assured, even in marriage, that the sex act is an expression of intimate, faithful love. When something is grossly out of kilter in a marriage, they usually require it to be put right before considering the marriage bed.

Sex has great power to energize men, women, and their marriages, but when it misfires, it can explode in our faces. Women can often tell us when it is going to misfire, so that we can get everything repaired first. Many men think nothing of having sex without regard to how it affects the relationship. They are forever prating about "conjugal rights," which, they point out, is a scriptural concept.

What wives say in return is a deeper truth than conjugal rights. They insist on conjugal love. They will not tolerate sex without love. Men may struggle with sexual desire, wanting relief from sexual temptations, but the challenge wives give back in return is only right. It requires men to convert sexual desire into building a love relationship. Men may interpret their wives' reluctance as rejection and insensitivity to their needs, but what women are really looking for is genuine acceptance, without which they feel used and abused. Love and sex are two different things, but we can learn to connect them so that both partners can go to bed happy, and get out of bed happy, too.

Question: In your mind, is sex an expression of intimate love toward your spouse most of the time?

Question: How do you usually interpret your spouse's refusal to make love with you? Is it possible that you misinterpret his or her refusal? Do you see it as rejection? Manipulation? Or evidence of some other motives deeper than tiredness or moodiness? Is it possible that a better love relationship could produce a better sex life, and a better sex life could draw you into a better love life? How would you begin to build into your marriage this God-given plan for sex?

9

Communication

Childhood can be a wargame. I (Doug) had a pretty tame childhood. Yet it was full of intrigues and plottings aimed at maintaining dignity among my peers. The world was full of other little people who were trying to prove their importance just as I was—though we all looked pitifully small and unimportant.

We cared little about the niceties of adult society, being more eager to prove ourselves against each other. The main weapons with which we fought for our self-importance were words.

Transformed by the Renewal of Our Mouths

Then one day Jesus came along and taught some of us that there is a higher calling in life than to work for our own importance. He taught us about faith working through love. We began to see that some of the polite conventions and niceties that adults observed in their conversation were not so stupid as they at first seemed. They were intended to

communicate honor—a type of love. When people feel honored, they show you their better side. Relationships become
enjoyable. Friendships blossom.

Honoring people became a new concept that we had to
work hard on. We learned a new language, the language of
honor. In the context of marriage we could learn this new
language every day. We could let honor infiltrate our words,
tone of voice, facial expressions, and gestures.

Antidotes to Poisonous Speech

The Bible says that we can best get rid of one pattern by
replacing it with another. For example, "each of you must
put off falsehood and speak truthfully to his neighbor" (Eph.
4:25), and "Do not let any unwholesome talk come out of
your mouths, but only what is helpful for building others
up according to their needs, that it may benefit those who
listen" (Eph. 4:29).

The Apostle Paul is applying the pattern of Christ to communication. He tells us to replace unhelpful patterns with
helpful ones. Paul says not only to stop administering poison, but also to administer the antidote, so that true healing can take place. Below, we list thirteen poisons that enter
into our speech. We also recommend the antidotes for each
of these poisons.

The Curse and the Roar

When we were children, some of us learned that an angry
outburst or a blast of cursing could intimidate and silence
others. We gained self-importance by showing everyone
that they should respect us and keep their distance. But
among adults, this pattern becomes counterproductive.

Those who turn to cursing and angry outbursts when
they feel attacked can unlearn this habit and learn the gentleness of Christ. Psychologists have disproved the old the-
ory that "venting" is a healthy means of healing all the emo-

tions that we have been "repressing." What the Bible says turns out to have been right all along. Angry outbursts and cursing do no good when a person habitually gives in to these patterns.

Carol Tavris reviewed hundreds of studies on anger. She found that expressing anger begets more anger, unless three conditions are met: (1) Your anger is aimed at the person who wronged you; (2) your anger is appropriate (not too much, not too little) for the offense; and (3) the person does not retaliate. Thus, unbridled expression of anger in an ongoing relationship is almost never calming "because parents, children, spouses and bosses usually feel obliged to agress back at you,"[1] so you not only feel more anger, you must deal with the other person's hostility, and worry about how (or if) you can repair the relationship later. The same is true in the forceful expression of other negative emotions.

Self-control is a fruit of the Spirit. God promises by the Spirit to build this character trait in us over a period of time if we will let him. That promise is a reliable hope for the long term.

But how about the short-term, when panicky anger rises up in you because your spouse seems to be attacking you? When you are going through that moment of panic, try this: Say to your partner, "I'm about ready to explode. I need to go for a walk to cool off. Please excuse me for a few minutes." As you walk off the stress, pray. Remember the basic fact of your faith: your worth does not depend on what other people say or do, but on the love of Christ proclaimed from the cross. Get back in touch with the merchant in search of fine pearls; remember that you are a pearl, a treasure in God's sight. Now God is calling you to be a fine pearl, to live out that calling, to rest in the knowledge of his honor, his valuing love. Also, your partner is a pearl of great value. He or she deserves to be treated with the same honor.

It is a rare partner who will not allow for a cooling off time when debate has grown angry or violent. To cool off is not to run away from responsibility or communication. It is a temporary reprieve, not a permanent escape. Your partner will likely appreciate your desire to avoid explosive, destructive anger, and will encourage you in this. The ten-minute walk is one way to apply the pattern of Christ to violent anger. The reprieve will also help both of you to look at your own destructive pattern of communication and to try a better way with words when you get back together.

Interrupting

Many people develop a habit of interrupting their partner. This creates dishonor. It says, "I don't want to listen to this," or "I've heard it all before."

To replace a pattern of interrupting, wait until your partner has finished a thought, then summarize in your own words what you heard. If you can convince your partner that you understand him or her, you will find your partner more eager to listen to you. "Everyone should be quick to listen, slow to speak and slow to become angry" (James 1:19). Listening communicates love because it says, "I value what you think and feel."

Often your partner does not know whether you are listening. A spouse who has learned that you probably are not listening must be convinced by proofs that you are changing. To repeat what he or she says in your own words is just the proof that your partner needs. See how quickly that attitude changes as you prove your listening love!

You can do more. Invite your partner to alert you whenever you interrupt and cut your partner off. Then, without defensiveness, ask forgiveness. Then go into a listening mode and discipline yourself to summarize what your partner says.

Paternalizing

Paternalism may take many forms and will invariably lead to the kind of "lording it over" people that Jesus so clearly denounces in such passages as Matthew 23:11–12, "The greatest among you will be your servant. For whoever exalts himself will be humbled, and whoever humbles himself will be exalted." Paternalistic speech includes the following:

- Ridiculing your spouse's opinions, ideas, struggles.
- Being distracted when he or she is speaking to you.
- Making jokes at your partner's expense.
- Saying "I told you so."
- Lecturing your spouse.
- Treating your partner like a child.
- Being rude to him or her publicly.
- Giving unasked-for advice.
- Leaving your spouse out when friends are present.
- Making your spouse feel stupid.
- Refusing to tell him or her of your day's activities ("A slave does not know his master's business," John 15:15).

Question: Stop for a minute and reflect on this list. Do any of these patterns creep into your communication with your partner? If the antidote to paternalism is honor—"outdo one another in showing honor" (Rom. 12:10, RSV)—check those paternalistic patterns that you discern in your speech and create alternatives that honor your partner. Be as specific as you can and visualize yourself speaking words of honor in situations where you normally have dishonored your partner.

Gossip

When you share marital secrets and disputes with friends or family members to gain allies, marital trust is violated.

You probably do not think about how it feels when your partner shares your secrets with other people. You only think about your distress and are seeking a way to relieve it. But you are purchasing your relief at the cost of your partner's trust, who will think twice the next time he or she confides in you.

Gossip can thrust a thick barrier between spouses. People who have destroyed trust with rampant gossip and broken confidences—pearls cast before swine—can begin slowly to build confidence back and regain trust. They must confess their mistake, ask forgiveness, and demonstrate repentance. It may take months or years to restore what has been lost, but the result is worth the struggle.

The antidote that restores and heals is prescribed in Matthew 18:15, "If your brother sins against you, go and show him his fault just between the two of you." Many couples routinely confide to friends marital issues that they are afraid to talk about with their own partners. This is an act of cowardice—and a recipe for disaster.

When your partner sees that you are gathering your courage to do the harder thing—to talk face to face about a disagreement—he or she will be more likely to trust you again.

Belittling

Many young couples learn that they can get a laugh from their friends by slamming their spouse. The spouse may even join in the laughing, but behind the hilarity, the spouse resents being slammed instead of honored. He or she may not mention this resentment for fear of being slammed about it as well. "Aw, quit being so sensitive! Can't you take a joke? Lighten up!" As a result, subtle and clever put-downs can damage a relationship more than you may realize, especially when you do this in the presence of other people.

Couples who have worked their way into this trap must learn the antidote—to be straightforward rather than clever. Instead of saying, "These steaks would make great shoes. Let's sell them to the Red Wing plant," the straightforward comment might be, "Darling, maybe we ought to try getting our meat at a different grocery store." The latter rejoinder may seem less fun. But fun at the expense of the spouse's feelings is not worth its price. Even better, if you are in the presence of people other than your partner, don't let criticism—humorous or straightforward—come out of your mouth. If you must criticize, save it until the two of you are alone.

The Sneer

A sneer can become so habitual that you don't recognize that you are using it. The antidote is to initiate other nonverbal communication that is incompatible with it.

It is difficult to maintain a sneer or other forms of hostile communication when you are tenderly touching your spouse or holding hands. You will immediately sense that one part of you is making war, while the other is waging love. Tenderly touch, and you'll find that there is a contagious infection that spreads from your hand to your face and wipes the sneer from it. Touching your spouse lovingly can overcome a sneer and other forms of nonverbal or verbal wargames. It may seem unnatural at first, but so are all habits when they are fresh and new.

Scolding and Lecturing

There is a place for loving confrontation, but scolding and lecturing are paternalistic and dishonoring to your spouse. It is possible to level with your partner without adding paternalism.

"You are a rotten husband. We oughta trade places for a day. Then you'd see what a real day's work looks like." This may seem like a way of leveling with your spouse. But leveling *with* your partner is different from leveling your partner. A more honest and honoring communication would be to say, "I'm exhausted. I've had it up to here with these kids. Steven is cutting teeth and he's been cranky all day. I've changed Chrissy's diaper four times today if I've done it once. I need a break. Could you *please* play with these kids while I get dinner, or I'm going to go insane."

The Freeze-Out

The freeze-out, and its cousin "the cold shoulder," are effective ways to guard your dignity, but they are poor ways to handle anger or make spouses feel loved. To those who use the freeze-out in response to anger, the Apostle Paul would say, "Do not let the sun go down on your anger." It is one thing to say "I need to go for a walk before I explode" and cool down for ten minutes. It is another to let a whole day pass without dealing with an issue or controversy. Soon coldness creeps into the relationship.

The answer to coldness is planned prime-time dialogue, an hour or two planned into your schedule when you can wrestle with the issues that have come between you. If bedtime is not a good time for this, plan a better time. Let relational winter give way to spring.

Carla and I find that prayer is hampered when we have outstanding issues, anger, and resentment from yesterday that we have not worked through. Since we have agreed to have an hour of prayer together at the beginning of each day, we occasionally find that we must work through unresolved issues before we can pray. Therefore, our prime time is sometimes between 5:00 and 5:30 A.M. When is yours?

Giving Orders

Some Christians have embraced a "chain of command" structure in family relationships. The idea behind the hierarchy is this: if the husband is the head of the wife, then the husband should give the orders and the wife should submit and obey.

Some Scriptures may seem to justify this idea, yet Ev and I believe that in some situations it violates the spirit of the love commandment. It can lead husbands to lord it over their wives, a pattern contradicted by Matthew 23:1–12, Ephesians 5:21, and 1 Peter 3:7. These verses say that submission is a two-way obligation under Christ. The implied devaluing of women created by the chain of command system often causes resentment that can break marriages apart.

We believe that when Paul called the husband "the head of the wife" (1 Cor. 11:3), he was referring to a man's initiative, not the right of command. God calls husbands to take initiative in fulfilling the love command and in being leaders in matters of faith. Most women look for leadership from their husbands and would gladly encourage it, but women rightly resent husbands who command them, because ordering people around is not the pattern of Christ.

The antidote is for each partner to treat the other as "an heir with you of the gracious gift of life" (1 Peter 3:7)—a prince and a princess under the lordship of Christ. If you find that you have developed the habit of ordering your partner around, you can unlearn that habit by frequently asking your partner, "What do you think about . . . ?" This is an invitation to share the rulership and to show honor.

Name-Calling

Names can be employed to honor or to dishonor, to alienate or to endear. I (Doug) have called my wife "my speckled fawn" because her freckles and red hair are dear to me. I call one daughter "Wizzy-giggles," and another "Blonde bombshell."

And I (Ev) call Kirby my "Little Princess," after Antoine de Saint Exupery's *Little Prince*, who in the novel was a master communicator who taught the novel's narrator to communicate, like Kirby taught me. Endearing names are the antidote to the dishonoring habit of name-calling.

Public Shaming

Scolding and nagging in public doubly dishonors. They patronize and shame a spouse. If you have developed this habit, undo the damage to your partner's worth by verbally honoring him or her in public. (In fact, it is a good idea to honor your partner in public regardless of whether you ever dishonor him or her.)

"My wife has taken over the checkbook duties in our house, and, as it turns out, she's better at it than I am." "Steve got a raise today. His boss thinks his work is the best hope for turning a profit this year."

Publicly bragging on a spouse can heal years of hurts from public humiliation. Make it your policy never to allow yourself a negative word about your partner.

Psychologizing

Psychologizing degrades people. The antidote to this habit is to allow them to tell you what is going on inside. Do this by probing for the feelings behind their words. Suppose your spouse says, "I don't want to spend Christmas with your parents this year." Instead of saying, "That's just because my parents tell you what no one else has the guts to say," you could ask, "Do they make you feel uncomfortable?"

The reply might be, "Yes, to be honest, they do. I feel like they never have accepted me."

"What makes you feel that way?"

"Well, remember when . . ."

By posing nonthreatening questions, your spouse may well examine his or her feelings in a new way, because you asked caring questions without violating your spouse with invasive, belittling insights.

Changing the Subject

Like interrupting, changing the subject is a way to keep from losing an argument. But if you have accepted the pattern of Christ, your goal is to pursue a disagreement until your partner feels heard and loved. Sometimes there will be no resolution of the issue itself. But because you hang in there without interrupting or changing the subject, you communicate caring love, and your spouse's attitude will soften.

It may be that you will end up saying, "I really don't know what to do about this," or "You really have backed me into a corner," or "I can see what you're driving at—what do you think we should do about it?" In each case, you admit to weakness, a position of humility that requires you to trust God rather than your own clever strategies for winning arguments.

Question: What would it cost you to apply the antidotes we suggest? Make a personal decision to try one of these in the area most needed.

Faith working through love, when it permeates all our communications, verbal and nonverbal, softens hearts by building honor. By facing up to our bad communication habits, we can open the door to a new kindness and gentleness, which will create an environment of love and security. In this environment, the issues of married life—money, sex, in-laws, children, vocations, vacations, and chores—are more easily solved, because we have developed ways of strengthening each other to solve them.

10

Conflict Management

All marriages have conflict. But conflict can be either mismanaged or managed.

There are two ways of mismanaging it: by avoiding issues that might lead to conflict; and by using conflict to destroy each other, rather than to emerge into a higher plane of awareness.

If we believe in God, then we must recognize that his point of view is higher and broader than ours. His thoughts are not our thoughts, his ways are higher than our ways. He sees every picture in its entirety and knows us fully. We know in part and we see only in part. Much conflict occurs in marriage because we do not have as complete a picture as God does.

A Personal Example

Some of the most frequent areas of conflict my wife and I (Doug) have these days are over the raising of our children, who are now teenagers. My wife often takes the view that we should limit the temptations to which our children are exposed, curtailing TV to two hours a week during school days, and limiting their friendships to those children whom we know and trust.

I maintain that we should talk with our children, model for them the kind of life we want them to live, teach them what is right, and then give them the freedom to make their own mistakes and to learn from them. Hopefully, when they get into a mess, they will be able to come to us and talk about it. We can help them learn from the messes they get into.

Carla is not sure that my way is in our children's best interest. She sees more clearly than I do a parent's protective role. I see more clearly our training role. The differences between us produce conflicts—especially when our teenagers go to the video store to rent a movie. Carla is more strict about what may be shown on our TV screen, though at times I have put my foot down.

We have had many serious, even heated, conversations about this subject. Both of us feel that the future of our children is at stake. We love our children very much, and our conflict is all the more heated because of that love. If we were apathetic people, we would never have conflicts. Because of our love, we have fresh conflicts every time our children bring home a new friend or video.

The important insight that we have come to through all of this is that both of us are limited in our perception. God is using each of us to open the eyes of the other to a more complex awareness than what we started with. To wit: the role of a parent must include both protection and training. We must protect our children from influences that they are not ready to handle yet. We must also train them and talk with them about the worldly influences that they can handle. By listening to each other throughout these conflicts, we are growing to a greater maturity, a broader understanding of our calling as parents.

In this, we are discovering the pattern that the Apostle Paul describes "Speaking the truth in love, we will in all things grow up into him who is the head, that is, Christ" (Eph. 4:15).

Areas of conflict are the acid test of our communication. They are the areas in which we find out whether or not we have learned the Christian principles described throughout this book. The practice of faith working through love in our communication may seem rather academic until we reach an area of conflict. Suddenly we realize it's sink or swim! We *must* give up destructive communication patterns or perish.

Christ or Compromise?

Many people speak of working through our conflicts to a compromise. It may be that compromise is all that is possible in certain situations. But Ev and I believe that through conflict, we may gain something of the higher awareness of what God wants. He challenges us to move beyond our limited awareness, brought on by our limited experience, and to see a situation more as he sees it. Speaking the truth in love is aimed, not at reaching a compromise, but at growing up into Christ. His ways are broader and deeper than ours.

Husbands and wives are given a piece of God's insight to share with each other. If each spouse sees only the value of his or her own perspective, conflict will rarely produce good results. When both husbands and wives admit that they have only part of the solution and learn to listen to what the other is saying, they are more likely to profit from the conflict. Thus conflict can make us richer through Christ, and not just poorer through compromise.

Question: What are your areas of persistent conflict? List them. Is God using your spouse to open your mind to some

blind spot that you have been avoiding? Can you see some
validity in your partner's arguments? Have you told him or
her so?

Truth plus Love Equals Maturity

"Speaking the truth in love" is Jesus' formula for growing up into mature adults, loving spouses, and stable parents. This formula avoids two options that don't improve a
marriage: avoiding the truth in love, and speaking the truth
without love.

Don and Frieda have frequent conflicts over sex. Both
feel that their sex life is the least satisfying area of their
marriage. Frieda does not like to talk about it. She has an
old-world reserve about such things. She is embarrassed to
put into words her sexual longings for a more romantic and
meaningful sex life. She feels that Don is clumsy when it
comes to making love. She wishes—for example—that he
would take a shower before love-making, that he would do
more to stimulate her sexually, and so on.

If she were to put these thoughts into words, she might
find Don amenable. But she has never learned to talk com-
fortably about sex. She believes that talking about it would
take the mystery out of it—would make it plain and common. Besides, she is baffled about what terminology to use
and finds it easier to use no terminology at all.

As Don senses his wife's reluctance to talk about and
enjoy sex, he grows disillusioned about the marriage bed.
"I don't suppose you'd want to make love tonight?" he says,
almost daring her to say yes. "Why am I the one who always
initiates lovemaking?" he fumes to himself. Frieda is never
the initiator.

Don becomes cynical about his marriage. He calls his
wife "Frieda the Frigidaire." He hopes to shock his wife into
a change. But speaking the truth without love only con-
vinces her that sex is a subject full of pain that must be

avoided at all costs. Inwardly Frieda longs for a romantic evening with her husband, where she is dressed in her sexiest lingerie and Don isn't angry with her. She would like to tell him what excites her, what she wishes him to do for her, to tell him the truth of what she longs for. But she can't—or so she tells herself. She is afraid of offending him, of being laughed at, of being embarrassed, of losing the sense of the sacredness of sex that she still possesses.

Don and Frieda must somehow learn to talk about this area together, *lovingly and frankly*. It is the pattern of Christ—speaking the truth in love.

> **Question:** Look at the list that you compiled in the previous question. As you have dealt with conflict in the past, did you have a tendency either to avoid, or to be destructive in conflict? In which area are you the more likely to fall short— in truth-speaking or in expressing yourself lovingly?

A Process for Conflict Management

We suggest a four-step process for resolving issues that erupt into conflict. Couples who carefully put their feet on each of these four "bases" are the most likely to hit home runs in conflict resolution.

First Base

Both partners define the problem in writing. You will never arrive at a solution until you have agreed on what the problem is. A couple can talk in circles for hours because each believes that the problem is something different from what the other believes.

It will help to write down the problem, then compare notes with your partner. Discipline yourself to two or three sentences, being concise and specific. For example, "Harry needs to stop being such a jerk" is not specific enough. (It is also not a way of speaking the truth in love because it merely indulges in name calling.)

Doris files that thought away, takes up her notebook, and writes: "Harry has spent a lot of our money on gambling, and we don't have enough money left for basics." That is a concise statement of a problem.

Writing in his notebook, Harry states the problem his way, "Doris, you nag me too much. I don't like being around you when you are like that. It's more fun to play poker with Fred, Mitch, and Buddy."

Each looks at the problem differently. But as they state the problem in concise terms, each is able to get to first base in managing it.

Second Base

Each spouse identifies the partner's position. Often, we get so consumed with our own view that we cannot identify with our partner's view. We must spend some time finding out clearly where our partner stands.

Harry has to find out some answers. Does Doris really have it in for him? Is she jealous of his friendships with "the guys?" Does she want him to spend no time with them at all? Is she turning into a middle-aged nag? Are her concerns purely financial? What does the checkbook say at the bottom line?

As he probes with discreet questions—"why don't you want me playing poker anymore?"—he begins to determine that her concern is strictly for finances. She is nervous and resentful of the amount of money he is losing, and would feel differently if his friends found some other way of spending their time. Harry admits to himself that, since he has let Doris handle the household finances, he has been careless about money. In fact, he has no idea how deeply his gambling has jeopardized his household's solvency. He has not looked at the checkbook in months.

Doris equally needs to more clearly identify Harry's position. He is not addicted to gambling *per se.* He bitterly resents his wife's intrusions into his friendships with his pals, which predate his marriage. He believes that Doris is trying to keep him from having a good time. That is his position.

Third Base

Each spouse identifies the interests behind the spouse's position. What is your spouse interested in preserving or attaining? Why is this matter so important to your partner?

Harry discovers that his wife is truly fearful about losing their money. He learns that she is not jealous of his friendships, even though he sometimes interprets her behavior that way. As he thinks about her concern, he realizes that the checkbook is indeed looking pretty sick and that her concern is well founded. He gulps twice and does some hard thinking about what they need to cut back on to keep from going more deeply into credit card debt.

Doris sees that her fear has made her unpleasant to be around. She is hurt by Harry's statement about her nagging, but she realizes that what he says is true. She has grown nagging and insistent. She realizes that she is not handling the money and gambling problem very well. She has tried to lecture Harry—sometimes in the presence of his friends—and to order him around. Lately Harry has been avoiding her, and her way of dealing with the problem has added to the deterioration of their relationship and of their ability to solve the problem. Because of her nagging and lecturing, she has made gambling almost a matter of conscientious objection to her husband. While trying to steer him from it, she has actually pushed him farther into it. Doris sees that she must respect her husband's integrity. Pushing never draws anyone closer. Pushing creates distance, and that is what has happened with Harry.

Each partner now better understands where the other one is coming from, each *identifies* and *identifies with* the other's interests.

Home Plate

Both spouses create a solution adapted to their interests. Harry recognizes that his gambling is irresponsible—a throwback to youthful days when he was footloose and fancy free. He should be moving on now, taking more responsibility for his wife and daughter. He is a Christian, and he believes that gambling, while not countermanded by specific Scriptures, does not treat God's resources productively or maturely.

Doris realizes that her own lack of faith has created fear, which has caused her to deal unhelpfully with her husband. Though her concerns are well founded, she decides to express her concerns differently. She is happy to see that Harry is willing to talk about options. He seems to recognize the validity of her concerns as he never has before. Together, they decide to establish a household budget, at least until the checkbook isn't so checkered with red and black ink. Harry decides to find other ways to have fun with his friends. Doris encourages him in this. Both bring their faith to bear upon their household finances. They pray about the matter together. They soon realize that they haven't been mature in Christ about the way they communicate. But they are now ready to try more straightforward, nonmanipulative, and loving ways of communicating their concerns to each other.

Thus their solution has covered three areas that will affect their interests: Harry's pastimes with his friends, the household finances, and future ways of problem-solving and conflict management. Harry has heard Doris's interest in more financial responsibility, which heals the anxiety that drives her to nag him about his friends. He has moved beyond his own concerns to recognize that both of them will suffer if they don't deal with the financial issues. Doris has identified Harry's interest to keep his relationships with Fred, Mitch, and Buddy, and is allowing him the space to continue those friendships.

If they hadn't gone through the four-step process, they might have come to a partial solution, but not as complete a solution as they attained. Or they might have come to no solution at all.

> **Try It!** Examine an area of frequent conflict. Move through each of the four steps. Don't skip the writing. As millions of people have discovered during Marriage Encounter weekends, writing "love letters" is a valuable way of cutting through negative patterns of speech and nonverbal communication. You can't sneer with your pencil! Many ways of destroying your partner's worth are set aside when you communicate by the written word. Take care, too, not to skip steps. That is like failing to put your foot on a base as you circle around toward home plate. When you do that, you can't score a home run.

11

Cognition

One of the most subtle causes of marital unhappiness comes from the place we least expect it—our thought life. Nobody ever began a marriage counseling session by saying, "We've got our thinking all wrong! Our problem is that we have negative cognition." But consider the following illustration of a sort of problem that counselors find remarkably frequent.

The Power of Negative Thinking

All her life, Holly cherished a conviction about men. "Men only want one thing. Sex. Also, they are high-and-mighty and egotistical. They don't know the first thing about kindness and decency." Holly had good reason for believing this way about men. All the men she had known, especially her father and brothers, fit this stereotype and have continued to support it.

Holly began to take an interest in a man whom she hoped would be different. Steve was a shoe salesman and a Christian. Courtship was a wonderful experience for both, and they soon got married. Their first years of marriage were happy. Steve and Holly went to church together. Their marital problems were minor, and they seemed to be doing well together.

Steve, however, had two failings that had gotten a hold of him during his pre-Christian, bachelor days: alcohol abuse and pornography. He hid these problems from Holly as best he could, being embarrassed about them because they did not fit with his professed Christianity. Steve believed that his bad habits should disappear all by themselves when he became a Christian. He did not recognize that virtually all Christians have carnal habits that remain from their pre-Christian days and that they have to "crucify" or "put to death by the Spirit" those habits, through faith in Jesus. Steve did not know how to confess sin, how to seek prayer from other Christians, how to develop relationships in which he would put to death his old habits. So he continued the bad habits, growing more and more guilty and upset with himself as he did.

One day, Holly discovered Steve's bad habits. She found a stash of pornography hidden in their basement. Also, Steve would stop by the tavern on his way home from the store. She often smelled liquor on his breath.

Holly might have lovingly confronted Steve about these things, hoping to help him overcome his problems. If she had been a sympathetic helper to her husband, she might have helped Steve.

But Holly was so shocked about the pornography that she couldn't see her role in loving Steve out of this old habit. Steve's alcohol, too, reminded her of her father and brothers, for all of them drank heavily and abused her when they drank. So Holly immediately thought, "Steve's no different from all the other men I've ever known. He just covered it up for a little while. He's an unreliable beast like all the rest. He only wants one thing, sex, and he hid his true nature to get it." Her thoughts traveled a well-worn path, based on her experience prior to marriage. At that point, her mental image of Steve began to change. She saw him as almost a reincarnation of her brothers and father. She compared him to them. Her experience of them colored her way of looking at Steve.

One day, she had a dream. Steve was behind her with a whip. She was bound with ropes, while Steve drove her along. She awoke, convinced that Steve was a beast and that she would never be happy with him.

Holly's mind had played tricks on her, but because her dream seemed so real, it was difficult for her pastor to convince her of this. He urged her to give Steve a chance to show his love, to overcome his problems, to grow to maturity in Christ. Holly had difficulty breaking free from the belief that she would always be victimized by men. She had to retrain her thinking; she had to focus on God's promises.

Below, we will describe how this retraining might work.

The Problem: Wounded People Expect Bad Things

Thoughts like Holly's can have a big impact on a marriage. People who have often been wounded may have negative expectations about each new person they meet. These negative expectations lie hidden from view in a marriage as long as the partner fulfills basic expectations and desires. But a crisis, such as a perceived betrayal, hurt, or revelation of some hidden character trait will trigger those hidden thoughts. The thoughts themselves then push away the hope, faith, and love of Jesus.

This is a form of prejudice—a way of prejudging people based on other people we have known who remind us of them. These habits are often subconscious; we are not aware of them. We also aren't aware of how unfair it is to let our perceptions of some people affect our expectations of others. Yet, because our minds are working subconsciously, we often do not recognize the unfairness of our judgments.

Three Quirks of Thinking

Negative thinking commonly takes three paths that affect marriage. First, we habitually *attribute blame* to our spouse for a problem. Second, we bring to our marriage *negative expectations about the marriage* or about the opposite sex. These can become self-fulfilling prophecies. Third, we bring *assumptions about marriage*, which may not be negative in themselves, but can lead to negative thinking when the assumptions prove untrue.

Attributions of Blame

Jane sensed that the romance had gone out of her marriage. She blamed this on John's workaholism. His priorities did not include quality time with her. Jane was right in seeing that John ignored her.

However, her attribution of blame was shallow and one-sided. It prevented her from seeing that she played her own part in the loss of romance, which was such an important part of her core vision for marriage. She had developed sloppy personal habits that turned John off. She nagged him. She made no effort to entice him or show him affection. She expected him to love her and woo her, and when he failed to do this, she blamed him alone.

One day, she spoke her mind. "John, you've changed. You're a different person now than the one I married. You're married to your business, not to me. You never take time for me and I'm sick of it. It's as though I'm not even here any more. I could vanish and you wouldn't even notice."

Jane never said, "Our marriage is empty and it's all your fault," but she implied it. Her approach immediately threw John into a counteroffensive—he blamed her in return. He accused his wife of the bad personal habits that had made her unattractive, of sexual coldness, of not reaching out to him, and of incessant nagging.

Both of these people were speaking the truth as they perceived it. Hidden in their perspective, though, was a mental habit of blame that made it difficult for each partner to hear what the other was saying. Jane was entitled to express her feelings of disappointment about her romantic core vision. John was entitled to express his desire for his wife to care for her appearance and to encourage her to make herself more attractive. Jane could have said, "I'd like to spend an evening with you in bed. What would I need to do to get you home from the office early tomorrow night." John could have bought his wife some beautiful new lingerie and said, "I'd love to see what you look like in this."

But either they both received too much secret pleasure in laying blame, or blame had become a stale unbreakable habit. Blame killed their productive thoughts before the seeds had a chance to take root in the mind of the other. Their hopes had no chance to grow into new patterns, new realities, new love. The poison of blame killed their hopes and buried the potential of new love.

Empathy

The antidote to blame is empathy. Empathy is an important ingredient in Christian love. Jesus had empathy when he looked on people who were "harrassed and helpless like sheep without a shepherd." Jesus had such empathy that he literally placed himself in our shoes, becoming fully human, experiencing our temptations, weaknesses, burdens, and fears. He didn't stay in heaven, the regal King of Heaven, blaming us for making a mess of God's world. He put himself in our place and then acted to free us from our sin.

Jane might have had empathy for John if she had seen John as Jesus sees him. She might have understood that

John's father was a workaholic, that John was doing what came naturally to him—imitating his father. She might have asked herself, "What am I doing to invite John to spend more time with me or to woo him into the pattern of Christ—faith working through love?" She might have. But she did not think of these options.

EMPATHETIC REPENTANCE

How do we gain empathy for someone who frustrates us, whom we find hard to love? We try empathetic repentance, a suggestion Larry Christenson makes in *The Christian Family*. We ask the Lord to reveal in us how we are practicing the very sin we are bothered by in the other person. We try to understand how the partner feels by identifying the same struggle in our own lives. We have found that we are rarely upset by someone else's sin. We are more often upset by our own sin, in response to others' sin.

In this we are taking stock of the words of the Apostle Paul, "You, therefore, have no excuse, you who pass judgment on someone else, for at whatever point you judge the other, you are condemning yourself, because you who pass judgment do the same things" (Rom. 2:1). The old adage is true: when we point a finger at someone, we point four fingers at ourselves.

In the above situation, Jane could ask herself, "Am I avoiding intimacy with John, allowing urgent trivia to distract me from loving him?" It may not be the business trivia that John uses to avoid Jane. Maybe it's soap operas, church work, childrearing, sewing projects, or phone conversations with her friends. Jane could ask God to reveal ways that she does the same things that her husband does. This would lessen her judgementalism and blame—and blunt the sharp edge on her voice, too.

When she then communicates her concerns about her marriage, she will speak lovingly and compassionately. She may say, "John, it's been ages since we went out on a date.

Could we go to the movies this weekend?" John may perceive that she wants to pull him out of a pattern, rather than to blame him for the pattern. Her approach will be more successful because it has proceeded from right thinking—thinking that has been cleansed of judgmentalism, condemnation, and blame.

Question: List each problem that you have blamed on your partner. Then in each area ask yourself two questions. (1) What other factors might be contributing to this problem—including factors in my own life? (2) Can I understand more deeply why the two of us are caught in this pattern? Do I struggle with the same failings that I have been blaming on him or her? Or can I identify similar struggles in the past so that I can sympathize with my partner's feelings now?

Negative Expectations

A second pattern of negative thinking takes the form of *negative expectations* about marriage. Negative expectations are especially common among those who have come out of broken homes or dysfunctional families. These expectations tend to generate a pattern in which the failings of parents become the failings of their married children.

Suppose Dad habitually said, "Women! Who can understand them! Next time I think about getting married to one, lock me up first!" As likely as not, a day will come when those words will seem prophetic to his son. They will bring doom and gloom to the one who remembers his father's proclamation about the inscrutability of women and the inevitability of marital pain. Negative expectations hinder marriages by discouraging people from hoping for better. Those who do not hope for better will never find it.

Sometimes negative expectations do not come from childhood remembrances but from concentrating too much on present problems. Most couples who have come to the point of seeking counsel do so because of the current pain they are giving each other. This pain is hard to ignore, and they have had many debates about how to get rid of it.

A by-product of this debate is that problems are magnified compared to the joys and rewards of marriage. When we concentrate on pain, the pain seems to grow worse. Soon, problems seem all-consuming and insoluble because they take up more and more of our conscious thoughts and talks. Blessing and happiness are forgotten. Pessimism consumes us because we spend so much time focusing on the negative. If you think that you are becoming overly focused on negatives and problems, try these antidotes.

The Miracle of the Thank You. Thanksgiving is especially valuable at times like this—and besides, it pleases God. Begin each day with thanksgiving. Thank God for what he has done for you both personally and maritally. Thank him in all circumstances, as the Scriptures advise you to do (Eph. 5:20). Thank him that he can turn every problem into a learning experience, using it to build your character (Rom. 5:3–5) Thank him that he answers prayer (James 5:15). Offer him a sacrifice of praise (Heb. 13:15). Thank him that he is able ultimately to deliver you from all of your afflictions when you persevere in faith (Ps. 34:17). Thank him above all for the cross of Christ, the unconditional love of God, the assurance of his forgiveness for both you and your partner, and for life everlasting (Rom. 8).

Your present trials, after all, are a fleeting turmoil that will soon pass away in the order of God's eternal purposes. Thanksgiving can help you put them into perspective and deliver you from the burdensomeness of life. The yoke of Jesus is not burdensome.

The Promises of God. Immerse yourself in and memorize the promises of God that apply to your situation. "I can do everything through Christ who gives me strength" (Phil. 4:13). "All things work together for the good of those who love God and are called according to his purposes" (Rom. 8:28).

God promised to bring hope to your despairing mind. He could have decided simply to bring to pass his will without making promises in advance. But because he was concerned about negative thinking, he gave his promises in advance to give all people hope and encouragement. On the other hand, if you don't let his promises enter your mind, they will do you no good. Dig into your concordance. Find the promises that apply to your unique situation. Memorize them and make them your own.

Take a Detour into Life. Plan relaxing, enjoyable times— dates, dinners, shared activities that will bring you closer together outside of heavy discussions about problems. Take on a project that the two of you can do together for someone else, if only to take the focus off of your own problems. Go on a mission trip. Ask God to give you a couple-ministry.

No Marathon Counseling Sessions. Limit your times of counseling and problem-solving to an hour and a half. You won't get much benefit beyond an hour and a half at one sitting. For every hour of problem-solving, reward yourself with an equal time of fun and relaxation. Work hard to implement what you learn in counseling. Then plan rewards for the work you've done.

Reminisce about the Good Times. Virtually all couples can think of some good times that they have shared lovingly with each other. Drag out old pictures, or slides, or love letters. Talk about your wedding or some positive experience of your honeymoon or early years. Remind each other of enjoyable hobbies, pastimes, or vacation places where you grew closer to each other.

Question: Would it be possible to rediscover some of the hobbies, vacation spots, shared activities, couple-ministries, or friendships that once brought you close together? Could you take them up again and let them have a renewed impact

on your relationship? Also, which of the above five suggestions might keep you out of the pit of a negative focus?

Assumptions about Marriage

A third type of negative thinking is the result of *myths
or mirages of marriage*—firmly held assumptions that may
or may not be negative in themselves, but that have a decid-
edly negative impact because they don't pan out. When they
don't pan out, they lead us to believe that something is
wrong with our partner, with us, or (less often) with me—
when in fact the assumption itself is off base.

All of us have a mental map of the terrain of a good marriage and the roads that lead to that beautiful country. We
use the map to help us identify the terrain and to negotiate
the roads. But sometimes—especially at the beginning of a
marriage—the map is based on wrong information. The terrain does not match the contours of the map, and the roads
only vaguely resemble the roads of a real marriage.

Who made this map? We did—sketched from the geo-
graphical information of parents, friends, Family Life class
teachers, soap operas, movies, books, and pastors. From
these assorted scraps of information, we pieced together
an understanding of marriage. But when our marriage does
not resemble the map in our head, we have a decision to
make. Either we must try to change the marriage to fit the
map, or we must change the map to fit the marriage.

In some cases, the map will guide us through forests that
merely obscure the lay of the land. In this case, we should
keep following the map, because it can prevent us from
wandering in circles. For example, the Bible gives us a pattern that we can cling to even when we feel lost in a forest
of conflicting emotions and perceptions. Faith working
through love is a reliable direction-finder that leads to life,
not only in marriage, but in all of life. Sometimes we must
cling to that pattern even when it does not seem feasible,

or when it seems not to lead us immediately to marital happiness.

There are other assumptions, though, that have proven to be myths and mirages to countless couples. Those who have clung to these assumptions have found that these promising looking paths do not lead to marital happiness and stability.

Kirby and I (Ev) were hiking in Mount Rainier one late afternoon. Ripe huckleberries beckoned us down a seemingly well-traveled path. Eventually, though, the path simply disappeared into the underbrush— an animal trail. We were lost on the mountain at dusk. Similarly, the following common assumptions may look enticing, but they can lead you astray. We list some of these assumptions that have often led nowhere for other couples.

1. "To prove his love, my husband must tell me he loves me several times a day."
2. "If I don't feel romantic with my wife, it means we aren't in love any longer."
3. "My husband should meet all my needs, especially my intimacy needs."
4. "My wife should support or agree with all my ideas."
5. "When I've had a bad day, my husband should sense it, and do something to cheer me up without my having to tell him to."
6. "My wife should not expect me to be courteous and polite to her. That's what marriage is all about—being yourself and not having to put on a show."
7. "My husband should be able to know how to stimulate me when we're making love. I shouldn't have to tell him how."
8. "My wife and I should do almost everything together as a couple if we are to maintain a happy marriage."
9. "I should be able to keep my partner from ever being unhappy."

10. "In a good marriage, partners will never have arguments."
11. "Whenever I'm ready to make love, my partner should be ready, too, if my partner truly loves me."
12. "Sex should always be spontaneous. We don't really love each other if we have to schedule sex in advance."

What makes these false assumptions so pernicious is that, when they turn out not to characterize our marriage, we conclude, "I don't have a good marriage," or "My spouse doesn't love me." Rather than changing the map, we begin to slow down on the road, convinced that the marriage is going nowhere.

A marriage that is pursuing God's pattern is certainly going somewhere good. But when we examine specifics, the end result may look quite different than what we expected at the start. Hollywood notions picked up from television, aphorisms inherited from parents, and whisperings we heard when we were ten must give way in the face of reality. If we ask God to show us how to apply the pattern of Christ, we will be most likely to have our expectations fulfilled, if not by our spouse, then by God himself, who is eager to fulfill his promises for those who trust him.

> Trust in the Lord with all your heart
>   and lean not on your own understanding;
> In all your ways acknowledge him,
>   and he will make your paths straight (Prov. 3:5–6).

Question: Do you hold to any of the dozen false assumptions we have listed above? Have you found them accurate? Are there perhaps other ideas about good marriages that you should give up because they are inaccurate? In giving up those ideas, must you give up all hope that your marriage can be a satisfying one?

12

Covenant and Commitment

Every Christian wedding includes a time for covenant-making. But covenants are a heavenly thing, hard for us to understand. Most people, when they enter a marriage covenant, do not understand what they are doing. They think in terms of contracts, not covenants.

The difference between a contract and a covenant is this. Covenants are based on unconditional love, the kind of love God has for us. Contracts are conditional, and merely human. Covenants are permanent agreements, like adopting a child. Contracts are tentative, like taking in foster children.

Adoption versus Foster Children

When Carla and I (Doug) adopted a girl in 1971, we entered into a permanent arrangement. We were challenged to love a little person who may or may not have loved us in return. This was a covenant. It was permanent and unconditional. We didn't say to the adoption agency: "We'll take this child, then we'll see how things work out. If we don't like this one, maybe we could try another one." We could say this in a foster-child agreement. But adoption is a covenant—permanent and unconditional.

Covenants are God's plan for families. All children need a mother and father who will love their children unconditionally. They develop their self-worth accordingly. Contractual relationships create rejection, even though they are more convenient. Rejection scars deeply and can cause permanent damage. God designs families as environments where we are loved unconditionally. That is why he recommends covenants, not contracts.

Some people think that the permanence of marriage is a curse, a prison. Actually, it is designed to be a blessing and a challenge, an environment where we learn to give and receive unconditional love.

Accepting God's Covenant

God revealed a covenant-making love in the covenants he made with Noah, Abraham, King David, and the Church. He showed throughout the ages that his divine love is utterly faithful, not tentative.

Jesus established a "marriage" with us, to be consummated at the marriage supper of the Lamb, when Jesus returns at the end of the age. He is preparing the Church as a bride. In getting engaged to this bride, he formed a covenant. He offered his love unconditionally and permanently. Of course, we can still refuse and abuse that love and thus cause him pain by rejecting him. That was his risk, but he was willing to take that risk.

This covenant happened unilaterally. As if he were adopting a baby, God decided to offer us love without asking what we thought about it. But that didn't mean that he didn't want us to respond to it. As the Apostle Paul wrote, "he died for all, that those who live should no longer live for themselves but for him who died for them and was raised" (2 Cor. 5:15).

When we respond to God's love by surrendering our lives to him, we enter into a covenant. People who do this find that they can sense a love relationship growing with Jesus. Jesus senses that they are no longer merely trying to use him to get what they want. He reveals himself to them more fully because he knows that their love is genuine.

Before we have surrendered our self-centered ambitions, all relationships tend to be subjected to them. We learn to use and abuse people. We manipulate people and God. Manipulation leads to stress and unhappiness.

When we've had enough of that, God gently invites us to step through a doorway. When we surrender to God every ambition, need, and desire, we can receive peace and joy from the Holy Spirit.

I crossed that threshold in 1972 during my second year as a pastor. Though all along I had counted myself as a Christian, I had not truly given my life to God. I was trying to cleverly manipulate God and other people so that I could be a success in my profession. When Carla, from time to time, made demands on me that interfered with my ambitions, I reacted with anger and resentment. At other times, other people seemed to keep me from success, but I was determined to prove myself in my chosen career. Professional success was my goal. Pursuing success in the Church (as opposed to a business) did not make it any less self-centered.

Within two years, I became a nervous wreck. I wasn't happy. Nor was Carla. Nor, I am sure, was God. Even in the ministry, I was trying to save my life, and I was losing it.

But through the help of a friend, I surrendered those ambitions to God. I said, "God, I'll be a ditch-digger if that is what you want." I laid down my life. It was death to self, the turning point in my life. I accepted the covenant God made with me: "Seek first his Kingdom and his right-eousness and all these things will be given to you as well" (Matt. 6:33).

Immediately, God released me from white knuckles and ulcers. He gave me peace. He came close. I sang to him, communicated with him. While there have been difficulties in my life since then, the general drift of my life has been upward into genuine fulfillment. I gave my life to him and he has been giving it back to me dusted off, polished up, and healed, to use me in his own way. Slowly but surely I have been released from the conviction that if I don't look after myself, no one else will.

The Act of Surrender

We grow in the personal knowlege of God as we learn this principle of personal surrender. The wild stallion does not know the caress of the master's son, nor does he enjoy the lump of sugar from the master's hand. He must be tamed first. The stallion must surrender his will, learn to listen to the master's voice, and not imagine that the master is subject to the stallion's whims. Once the will is surrendered, there will be quiet walks down country lanes, and precious moments between horse and rider.

If we don't surrender our will, the relationship Jesus offers us is wasted. We are too busy prancing about empty fields to be friends with God.

Your attitude should be the same as that of Christ Jesus, who, being in very nature God, did not consider equality with God something to be grasped, but made himself nothing, taking the very nature of a servant, being made in human likeness. And being found in appearance as a man, he humbled himself and became obedient to death—even death on a cross. Therefore God exalted him to the highest place (Phil. 2:5–9).

Jesus entered into the covenant with us by surrendering his will to what the Father wanted. Likewise, we accept and take part in that covenant by surrendering our will. Self-surrender is the doorway to covenant love.

God calls us into a covenant both with him and with our spouse. In a covenant, we can give each other unconditional love. Apart from the covenant, there is an unspoken agreement between spouses: "If you do this for me, I'll do that for you." This is not unconditional love, and it is permanent only if both people are entirely trustworthy.

Question: When you got married, which idea about marriage did you have in mind—covenant or contract? Has your idea changed over the years?

Why Are Covenants So Hard to Keep?

Before we can seriously consider covenant love, we must deal with our self-centeredness. We must let God do major surgery on us. Our subtle manipulation to get our way undermines covenants. Therefore, we must take seriously what Jesus said about crucifying self.

Jesus is the best marriage counselor. He sees more deeply than all the others. His advice for complete healing is more radical and penetrating than others' advice. *Others say*, "You just need a little work with budgets, a little sexual adjustment, and a week's vacation." *He says*, "You must deny yourself, take up your cross and follow me. For whoever wants to save his life will lose it, but whoever loses his life for me will find it" (Matt. 16:24–25).

If we examine ourselves carefully, many of us honestly feel that we don't need anything as radical or as blatantly Christian as all that. We minimize our difficulties. "Our marriage isn't too bad," we insist. "It's nothing we can't handle, now that we've had a chance to talk with the pastor a bit." We're hoping for a $6.00 prescription to heal us.

But Jesus says we're only postponing the inevitable—major surgery.

Major Surgery

Jesus entices us to die to self, to "crucify the flesh," to "put to death the deeds of the body by the Spirit." If this sounds like major surgery, it is. Marriage confronts us with our need for the surgery, and the longer we put it off, the longer we draw out the agony of our sickness. We have seen couples suffer for years by avoiding this spiritual and marital surgery.

Jesus asks that we give up our hopes, ambitions, needs, and desires in favor of *his* hopes, ambitions, needs, and desires. That's like a brain exchange or a heart transplant. Who would volunteer for such a thing? This doesn't even sound like good news. "Isn't Christianity supposed to be good news? How is crucifying your self good? Why would we give up our fondest desires for those of Jesus?"

For two reasons.

Jesus Beckons Us to Lay Down Our Lives

First, Jesus' death and love draw us into self-sacrifice and heroism. Here is how this works.

Consider that great saint, Maximilian Colbert. While interned in a prison camp he learned that a fellow prisoner was condemned to die. Seeing that the man was not ready to die, Colbert willingly offered his own life as a substitute. The offer was accepted. Maximilian Colbert was executed.

If you were the man who had escaped this death sentence, how would you feel? After that costly rescue, would you be content to live a life of lying, cheating, fornicating, and chasing money? Wouldn't you try to make something good of your life so that the one who died for you would not have died in vain?

Jesus' death was a sacrifice for our benefit. God gave the Holy Spirit, the Bible, and the sacraments of the Church to keep alive the remembrance of his death, to reawaken it with each passing generation so it can continue to provoke us to love and to heroism. The dying Jesus keeps on saying from the cross, "Don't waste my death. Let it touch you. Let it make you great. I died for you. Will you die for me?"

We can lay down our self-interest and take up God's interests because of Jesus' noble act. We love because he first loved us. The covenant he made with us invites us to make a covenant with him and with our spouse.

God Taketh and God Giveth Back

The second reason for giving up our self-interest is this. Jesus said that if we lose our lives for him, we will find them. When we give to God something we desire, God often dusts it off, fixes it, polishes it, and gives it back better than it was before. Of course, he only does this when we desire what is truly in our best interest.

By contrast, when we cling to something too tightly, we crush it. Our expectations for our marriage are like that. We can try too hard, grip them too tightly, and crush them in our grasp. Often, when we see our fondest desires eluding us, what God wants us to do is to let go of them before we crush them. "He who tries to save his life will lose it. He who loses his life for me will find it." Again, we see that an act of surrender is required.

Question: Is there any particular need or desire related to your marriage that God especially wants you to give up to his care and keeping? Look especially at persistent unmet needs and areas of perpetual conflict.

A Joshua Memorial

If you and your spouse both want to accept or renew your covenant love, why not build a "Joshua memorial?" After Joshua crossed the Jordan River, God said, "Take up twelve stones from the middle of the Jordan . . . and put them down at the place where you stay tonight . . . to serve as a sign among you" (Josh. 4:3, 6).

When a couple takes significant steps in creating or renewing covenant love, they deserve to celebrate the steps they have taken. They have crossed their own Jordan, and have arrived on the shores of their own promised land.

How do you establish a Joshua memorial? Not necessarily with heaps of stones, unless you have a personal liking for stoneheaps. One couple went on a ski trip each winter to celebrate the completion of counseling that had a permanent impact on their marriage. Another took a vacation away from the children each year. Another bought a box in which they each placed a small scroll stating their desire to make their marriage a reflection of God's ever-faithful love for his Church. They placed this box in a prominent place where they were frequently reminded of their covenant commitment.

> **Assignment:** If it seems right to both of you, think of a Joshua memorial that would be a fitting remembrance of steps you have taken to renew your marital love and affirm your covenant commitment to each other.

The Pattern Has No Limits

In marriage, God challenges us to attempt a deeper faith and love. Lessons learned in the privacy of marriage can bring life to other corners of our world, beyond the privacy of our household. They bring new love and Christian witness at work, at school, at church, and in our neighborhood, for we are now empowered to practice the pattern of Christ wherever we go. We have put our self-will in subjection to Christ where the test runs deepest—at home. Now he will use our obedience to bring a refreshing love elsewhere. We can become the hands, feet, and mouth of Christ, because we have in some small way died to self, and decided to live out his pattern: faith working through love.

Notes

Chapter 1: *The Valley of Trouble*

1. The statistical probability that a first marriage will end in divorce still stands at about 55 percent. The percentage of marriages that today have thus far ended in divorce is much lower—about 25 percent.

2. Dan Coates. 1991. America's Youth: a Crisis of Character. *Imprimis*, 20 (9): 3.

3. David G. Benner. 1992. *Strategic Pastoral Counseling.* Grand Rapids: Baker Book House, 133.

Chapter 9: *Communication*

1. Carol Tavris. 1982. *Anger: The Misunderstood Emotion.* New York: Simon and Schuster, 136.

Chapter/Section	NAEYC Early Program Standards and Accreditation Criteria	Developmentally Appropriate Practice (DAP) in Early Childhood Programs Criteria	International Reading Association 2010 Standards for Reading Professionals
The National Early Literacy Panel (p. x)	2.D.04, Language Development: Vocabulary development; 2.E.03, Curriculum: Nonverbal communication development; 2.E.04, varied opportunity; 2.E.05, writing opportunity; 2.E.06, phonological play; 2.E.07, letter recognition; 2.E.08, books and writing materials	I 1,4, Assessment; I 2 – 8, Planning curriculum; III 1 – 5, Book reading & motivation; IV 1 – 9, Writing; V 1 – 4, Planning curriculum; VI 1 – 5, Building knowledge & comprehension	2, Curriculum & Instruction; 5, Literate Environment
Language Use in Curriculum Areas (p. x)		I 1, Conversations; I 10-12, Vocabulary & word meaning; VI 1, Building knowledge & comprehension	2, Curriculum & Instruction
Goals for Children's Writing Development (p. x)	2.E.03, print familiarity; 2.E.05, multiple and varied writing experiences	IV 1 9, Writing	2, Curriculum & Instruction
Brain-Based Learning and Theme Instruction (p. x)	2.D.07, Language development: Varied discussion experiences	VI 1-5, Building knowledge & comprehension	1, Foundational Knowledge; 2, Curriculum & Instruction
CHAPTER 7: PROMOTING LANGUAGE AND LITERACY			
Providing Accurate and Specific Speech in All Content Areas (p. x)		I, Language & literacy; IV, Writing	1, Foundational Knowledge; 2, Curriculum & Instruction; 4, Diversity; & 5, Literate Environment
The Teacher—An Educator Who Interacts (p. x)			1, Foundational Knowledge
Scaffolding (p. x)	2.E.03, Cognitive curriculum: Connecting print words; 2.E.04, engaging conversations; 2.E.05, functional use of writing; 2.E.06, phonological awareness	I, II, III, IV, & V, Planning curriculum to achieve important goals	1, Foundational Knowledge & 2, Curriculum & Instruction
CHAPTER 8: DEVELOPING LISTENING SKILLS			
Questions to Ponder (p. x)	2.E.04, Cognitive curriculum: Connecting print words; 2.E.06, phonological awareness	1, Listening, speaking & understanding	2, Curriculum & Instruction
Critical Listening Activities (p. x)	2.E.04, Curriculum: Critical thinking activities	I, Listening, speaking & understanding	2, Curriculum & Instruction
Auditory Activities (p. x)	2.E.06, providing multiple and varied phonological opportunity to individual children	III, Phonological awareness	2, Curriculum & Instruction
Phonemic Awareness Skill (p. x)	2.E.06, providing multiple and varied phonological opportunity to individual children	III, Phonological awareness	
CHAPTER 9: CHILDREN AND BOOKS			
Illustrations (p. x)	2.E.04, Early literacy and curriculum: Differentiate from pictures in book	III, Phonological awareness	1, Foundational Knowledge & 2, Curriculum & Instruction
Reading Books to Young Children (p. x)	2.E.04, Curriculum: Programs with varied experiences and opportunities		2, Curriculum & Instruction
Culturally Conscious & Culturally Diverse Books (p. x)		II, Book reading & motivation	4, Diversity
Story or Book Dramatization (p. x)			2, Curriculum & Instruction
CHAPTER 10: STORYTELLING			
Storytelling and Literacy (p. x)			1, Foundational Knowledge
Storytelling Goals (p. x)	2.D.04, Language development: Using storytelling vocabulary development		1, Foundational Knowledge;
2, Curriculum & Instruction			
Themes and Story Structure (p. x)		I, Listening, speaking & understanding; V, Letter, word & print knowledge	
Storytelling with Young Limited-English Children (p. x)			4, Diversity
CHAPTER 11: POETRY			
Questions to Ponder (p. x)	2.E.02, Curriculum: Song, poetry for toddlers—words represent reality	III, Phonological awareness	1, Foundational Knowledge; 2, Curriculum & Instruction
Poetry and Early Reading Ability (p. x)	2.E.10, Early literacy: Identifying phonemes in varied activities including poetry	III, Phonological awareness	2, Curriculum & Instruction
Teacher Techniques (p. x)	2.E.06, Early literacy: Encouraging letter sound play with poetry	III, Phonological awareness	1, Foundational Knowledge; 2, Curriculum & Instruction
Sources (p. x)			4, Diversity
CHAPTER 12: FLANNEL (FELT) BOARDS AND ACTIVITY SETS			
Questions to Ponder (p. x)	2.D.04, Language development: Presenting books visually on the flannel board; 2.D.05, pairing set figures with words; 2.D.06, materials related to the physical world	I, Listening, speaking & understanding; II, III, Phonological awareness; VI, Building knowledge & comprehension	2, Curriculum & Instruction

(continues on page 606)